MEDIA, FEMINISM, CULTURAL STUDIES

Stepping Forward: Essays, Lectures and Interviews
by Wolfgang Iser

Wild Zones: Pornography, Art and Feminism
by Kelly Ives

Global Media Warning: Explorations of Radio, Television and the Press
by Oliver Whitehorne

'Cosmo Woman': The World of Women's Magazines
by Oliver Whitehorne

Andrea Dworkin
by Jeremy Mark Robinson

Cixous, Irigaray, Kristeva: The Jouissance of French Feminism
by Kelly Ives

Sex in Art: Pornography and Pleasure in Painting and Sculpture
by Cassidy Hughes

The Erotic Object: Sexuality in Sculpture
From Prehistory to the Present Day
by Susan Quinnell

Women in Pop Music
by Helen Challis

Detonation Britain: Nuclear War in the UK
by Jeremy Mark Robinson

Julia Kristeva: Art, Love, Melancholy, Philosophy, Semiotics
by Kelly Ives

Luce Irigaray: Lips, Kissing, and the Politics of Sexual Difference
by Kelly Ives

Helene Cixous I Love You: The Jouissance of Writing
by Kelly Ives

The Poetry of Cinema
by John Madden

The Sacred Cinema of Andrei Tarkovsky
by Jeremy Mark Robinson

Disney Business, Disney Films, Disney Lands
by Daniel Cerruti

Feminism and Shakespeare
by B.D. Barnacle

Luce Irigaray

Luce Irigaray

Lips, Kissing and the Politics of Sexual Difference

Kelly Ives

CRESCENT MOON

CRESCENT MOON PUBLISHING
P.O. Box 1312, Maidstone
Kent, ME14 5XU
Great Britain
www.crmoon.com

First published 1998. Second edition 2008. Third edition 2010.
Fourth edition 2013.
© Kelly Ives 1998, 2008, 2010, 2013.

Printed and bound in the U.S.A.
Set in Palatino 9 on 14pt.
Designed by Radiance Graphics.

British Library Cataloguing in Publication data

Ives, Kelly
Luce Irigaray. – (European Writers Series)
1. Irigaray, Luce, 1932 – Criticism and interpretation
I. Title
848.9'14'09

ISBN-13 9781861714510 (Pbk)

CONTENTS

ABBREVIATIONS

LUCE IRIGARAY

I	*The Irigaray Reader*
Je	*Je, tu, nous*
S	*Speculum*
TD	*Thinking the Difference*
Sex	*This Sex Which Is Not One*
EM	"Ecce Mulier?", in P. Burgard
ML	*Marine Lover of Friedrich Nietzsche*

JULIA KRISTEVA

K	*The Kristeva Reader*
DL	*Desire in Language*
R	*Revolution in Poetic Language*
TL	*Tales of Love*
PH	*Powers of Horror*
ACW	*About Chinese Women*
BS	*Black Sun*
SO	*Strangers to Ourselves*
QS	"A Question of Subjectivity"

HÉLÈNE CIXOUS

C	*The Hélène Cixous Reader*
NBW	*The Newly Born Woman*
BP	*The Book of Promethea*
EHC	"An Exchange with Hélène Cixous", interview, in V. Conley,

1991
Con   "Conversations", in S. Sellers, 1988
EF   "Extreme Fidelity", in S. Sellers,1988
DJ   "Difficult Joys", in H. Wilcox, 1990

M   *New French Feminisms*, Marks & de Courtivron, eds

They who dare all go forth blindly, without projects. No longer spell-bound by the fear of being without shelter. Unreservedly abandoning themselves to the unbounded open, holding nothing back. A flowering environment in which those who are free of all fear would be embraced.

Luce Irigaray, *Le Oubli de l'air*

Luce Irigaray

Some book covers of works by Luce Irigaray

PREFACE

This book is a study of the French feminist and philosopher Luce Irigaray, It employs parts of an earlier study of Hélène Cixous, Julia Kristeva and Luce Irigaray, who are called the 'holy trinity' of French feminism (D. Landry, 1993, 54). Before moving on to discuss Irigaray's work, I survey the work of these three French feminists. French feminism is often reduced to meaning the writings of this holy trio, while at other times it refers to criticism in the wake of Jacques Lacan, Jacques Derrida and Michel Foucault (these three male writers are sometimes seen as an equivalent of the Cixous-Irigaray-Kristeva trinity [J. Duran, 163]).

The trio of feminists/ philosophers/ speakers/ poets are extraordinarily enriching. Their writing is alive and they are not limited to having one or two things to say. Rather, they say a lot, about a lot. Sometimes they are outrageous, at other times they are incredibly, searingly poignant. Some feminists are suspicious of calling Hélène Cixous, Luce Irigaray and

Julia Kristeva 'radical': for Chris Weedon they are radical (Irigaray in particular [1987, 9]), but not for Stevi Jackson.[1] Does it matter? The works of Cixous, Irigaray and Kristeva have gone beyond such notions. With its mixture of male writers (Derrida, Lacan, Foucault) and certain female writers (Kristeva, Cixous, Irigaray, Monique Wittig):

> The boundaries of 'French feminism' are thus strangely constructed: some men fall within its definition, as do women who do not call themselves feminists, but those who have always called themselves feminists are excluded. (Stevi Jackson)[2]

In this book I do not work my way carefully and slowly through each stage of Luce Irigaray's career and writings. I do not offer in-depth analyses of every idea in Irigaray's *œuvre*. Rather, I hope to convey some the inspiration and excitement that her work instils. Irigaray annoys many feminists – her insistence on the body and biology, for instance, aggravates some theorists. Irigaray seems to frustrate people the most with her theory of the labial lips always touching, her notions of sexual difference, and so on. Emphasizing sexual difference or female essence, anti-Irigarayan critics claimed, detracted from the feminist fight for social and economic equality.

The big name cultural philosophers and critics, among whom Hélène Cixous, Luce Irigaray and Julia Kristeva are major players, publish in academic journals such as *Diacritics, Signs, Feminist Studies, Tel Quel, differences, Camera Obscura, Screen, Wide Angle, Yale French Journal, October, Social Text* and *Monthly Review.*

French feminism has been made more widely available in anthologies such as *New French Feminisms* (1981) and *French Feminist Thought* (1987). Before these appeared, however, few of the full-length works of French feminists had been translated into English. Only by about 1985 had Cixous, Kristeva and Irigaray been translated into English (J. Duran, 177). Further, the theorists themselves (such as Monique Wittig, Annie Leclerc, Cixous, Kristeva, Irigaray), do not class themselves as 'feminists', in the same way Anglo-American feminists do.

French feminism is part of a movement in criticism which exalts post-modernism via modernism. The 'classic' modernists are exalted by the 'classic' postmodernists: Gustave Flaubert by Roland Barthes, René Magritte by Michel Foucault, James Joyce and Antonin Artaud by Julia Kristeva, Stéphane Mallarmé and Antonin Artaud by Jacques Derrida, Jean Genet and Marcel Proust by Hélène Cixous.[4] Yes, the writers and artists most often enshrined by French intellectuals are also French; or they are celebrated artists and writers from the European canon (with artists and writers from Russia, Britain and Germany being favoured).

PART ONE

FRENCH FEMINISM

I

⊛

INTRODUCTION

LUCE IRIGARAY: BIOGRAPHY

Luce Irigaray was born May 3, 1932 in Belgium (some sources say 1930). So she's not strictly a *French* feminist. She studied at the University of Louvain; she worked on a master's degree in psychology at the University of Paris (1959-62); and at the Institut de Psychologie de Paris (1962). From 1962-64 she worked at the Foundation Nationale de la Recherche Scientifique in Belgium, and then at the Centre National de la Recherche Scientifique in Pars, where she eventually became Director of Research. She produced a doctoral degree in linguistics (University of Paris X at Nanterre, 1968), and in philosophy (University of Paris VIII, 1974). Irigaray was, famously, a member of the École Freudienne, presided over by Jacques Lacan. Irigaray's second dissertation (*Speculum de l'autre femme*) created some controversy among the members of the Freudian School, and Irigaray became an outcast from the École Freudienne. This was a key setback in her academic career: some critics have claimed that Irigaray 'has never enjoyed the scholarly recognition in France that she has earned on the international scene'.[1]

In the 1970s and 1980s, Luce Irigaray taught at Rotterdam, Bologna, Toronto and Paris, among other places. With books such as *Ce Sexe qui n'en est pas un, Et l'une ne bouge pas sans l'autre, Amante Marine: De Friedrich Nietzsche, Sexes et parentés, Sexes et genres à travers les langues* and *Le Oubli de l'air: Chez Martin Heidegger*, Irigaray became a major, international philosopher.

✤

Hélène Cixous, Luce Irigaray and Julia Kristeva all have different modes of writing. There are times when they are writing in the sober, measured tones of a cultural critic, philosopher or psychoanalyst. They have strident feminist voices (Cixous and Irigaray more than Kristeva). They have personal reminiscence modes. They have a relaxed, informal mode in interviews. And, most powerful of all, they have lyrical modes. Thus, Cixous, the most 'poetic' of the three, will break into a visionary, ultra-lyrical way of writing. In "Stabat Mater", Kristeva wrote passionately of her experience of childbirth:

> Nights of wakefulness, scattered sleep, sweetness of the child, warm mercury in my arms, cajolery, affection, defenceless body, his or mine, sheltered, protected. A wave swells again, when he goes to sleep, under my skin – tummy, thighs, legs: sleep of the muscles, not of the brain, sleep of the flesh. The wakeful tongue quietly remembers another withdrawal, mine: a blossoming heaviness in the middle of the bed, of a hollow, of the sea... (K, 171-2)

Luce Irigaray, too, changes – though less frequently than Hélène Cixous – from a critical to a lyrical form. Thus, in a piece such as "When Our Lips Speak Together", Irigaray will write poetic sentences such as '[k]iss me. Two lips kiss two lips, and openness is ours again.' This is the kind of phrase which never appears in most cultural theorists outside of quotation marks. One doesn't find Jacques Derrida, Jacques Lacan, Gilles Deleuze, Jean Baudrillard, Jean François Lyotard, Mikhail Bakhtin, Michel Foucault, Louis Althusser, Fredric Jameson, Roland Barthes or Jean-Paul Sartre writing 'kiss me' very often. Well, perhaps Foucault and Barthes said 'kiss me' in darkened hotel rooms – but not in scholarly books published by Minuit or Gallimard.

What marks Hélène Cixous, Luce Irigaray and Julia Kristeva apart from many cultural theorists and philosophers, then, is this personal, confessional and poetic way of writing, where they directly address the reader as the other, the 'you' in an intimate relationship. Jacques Derrida, Michel Foucault, Jean Baudrillard, Michel de Certeau, Terry Eagleton and Ramon Jakobson are rarely, if ever, this personal. Cixous, Irigaray and Kristeva, then, are more than simply cultural critics, shuffling between the café and the university library, lighting their pipes (Sigmund Freud) or chainsmoking cigarettes (Jean-Paul Sartre), or bitching about Amerika (any French intellectual), while they ponder on imponderables, chat about prostitutes and brothels with their cronies and write up the occasional philosophical paper.

Hélène Cixous, Luce Irigaray and Julia Kristeva are considerable poets as well as psychoanalysts and philosophers. Their writings have a tremendous *verve*, even when they are dealing with the arid heights of abstruse semiological theory. Kristeva, for example, in writing of childbirth in "Stabat Mater", foregrounds her own experience in ways which many masculinist cultural critics do not, would not, or could not. Kristeva very deliberately places her own experience of something very much in the province of 'women's experience' in a cultural theory essay. Of course, masculinist critics and writers have oft discussed sex, violence and death from 'first hand' experience, so to speak (Marquis de Sade, Georges Bataille, Jean-Paul Sartre and Michel Foucault), but for Kristeva the experience of motherhood decentres men and masculinist theory.

Feminist theorists and poets such as Hélène Cixous, Luce Irigaray and Julia Kristeva are valuable, then, precisely because they foreground experiences that have been sidelined or stereotyped for centuries.

Kristeva's account of childbirth knocks away conventional accounts, such as from traditional science and medicine, or from the early Christian 'fathers', such as St Augustine, who maintained, in the bizarre way of his, that we are all born between fæces and urine. The French feminists counter this demonization of female sexuality and make it a central part of their study. The effect of such foregrounding of female sexuality is disruptive and subversive. As Irigaray said in *This Sex Which Is Not One*: 'what is most strictly forbidden to women today is that they should attempt to express their own pleasure.' (I, 125)

Experience itself is not to be sidelined, as Elizabeth Grosz has suggested in *Volatile Bodies*, but is a useful issue in feminism: Grosz has drawn on the philosophy of Maurice Merleau-Ponty in this regard. However, experience is also culturally conditioned:

> Experience is not outside social, political, historical, and cultural forces and in this sense cannot provide an outside vantage point from which to judge them. Merleau-Ponty's understanding of the constructed, synthetic nature of experience, its simultaneously active and passive functioning, its role in both the inscription and subversion of socio-political values, provides a crucial confirmation of many feminists' unspoken assumptions regarding women's experiences. (94-95)

Hélène Cixous, Luce Irigaray and Julia Kristeva pull language apart and remake it. They often put words in parentheses and quotes, or split them up, or hyphenate them. Word plays such as 'specula(riza)tion' are common in their work. They parody classic texts and draw attention to hypocrisy and banality. They snuggle up close to classic philosophic texts and parody them in order to bring out the blind spots, repressions and hypocrisies. Irigaray uses mimicry and pastiche to interrogate philosophy; she has rewritten Friedrich Nietzsche and Sigmund Freud, much as Monique Wittig has reworked Dante Alighieri and Miguel de Cervantes, and Cixous has tackled Greek mythology, Freud and the *Bible*.

In particular, words such as *il* and *elle,* the gendering of French words, is central to their reworking of language and philosophy. This makes their writing particularly difficult to translate, because they are moving back and forth, continually, between received and ironic/ polemical treatments of language. Thus, translators and editors are forced to interject, and set words in square brackets [thus], in order to remind the reader of the original French text. Hélène Cixous and Luce Irigaray are the most playful in this respect: for this reason, their texts should always, ideally, be quoted in the French and in translation. However, as this is a study written in English, I have not assumed that readers can read French, so I have generally drawn on the English translations of Cixous, Irigaray and Kristeva that are available. Where possible, I have used the collections of writings or anthologies of Cixous, Irigaray and Kristeva (*The Hélène Cixous Reader* (Routledge), *The Irigaray Reader* (Blackwell) and *The Kristeva Reader* (Blackwell), as these are generally available. These are scholarly, well-edited selections of key works of Cixous, Irigaray and Kristeva. Unfortunately, many of the English translations of Cixous, Irigaray and Kristeva are published in less widely available editions (by University of Minnesota Press, Columbia University Press, Harvard University Press, Athlone Press and Cornell University Press). These are excellent editions, but Cixous, Irigaray and Kristeva have not been taken up by a mainstream publisher – their works remain available only in large or specialist stores.

French writers are specially prone to word games (and critics sometimes try to ape them, desperate to show off). The trouble with word games and puns is that they often come across as immature, pompous, and kinda pointless. Showy, self-conscious. 'Look at me! Look what I can do with L-Ah-nN^^Nn<>Goo-u[1234567890]-A-g-e.'

2

FRENCH FEMINIST POETICS: FEMINIST AND WOMEN'S ART

One of the problems that feminists have addressed with regard to women's art is: can there be a truly 'female' or 'feminine' or 'women's' art? Is art made by women (women's art) ever completely free of patriarchal influences, structures, forms? Can there be a women's art that exists in its own female space, away from patriarchy and masculinist ideas and experiences? Julia Kristeva is pessimistic on this contentious issue. For her, there has been no 'female writing' thus far in our culture. She said in 1977:

> If we confine ourselves to the *radical* nature of what is today called 'writing', that is, if we submit meaning and the speaking subject in language to a radical examination and then reconstitute them in a more

polyvalent than fragile manner, there is nothing in either past or recent publications by women that permits us to claim that a specifically female writing exists.[1]

In French feminism the text is primary, and a text can be 'feminine' regardless of who creates it. For Hélène Cixous a man can write a 'feminine' text (such as Jean Genet). In "Sorties", where Cixous provides a list of oppositions, the ones on the 'night' or 'feminine' side are the ones most often associated with poetry: 'mother', 'heart', 'sensitive', 'moon', 'night' and 'nature' (M, 90). For Cixous, most writing, by men or women, is masculine. She writes:

> Most women are like this; they do someone else's – man's – writing, and in their innocence sustain it and give it voice, and end up producing writing that's in effect masculine.[2]

The notion of '*écriture féminine*' of Luce Irigaray and Hélène Cixous, which's much discussed in feminist literary criticism,[3] is rejected by Monique Wittig. Wittig also rejects the notion of 'man' and 'woman'. For her, 'woman' is a historical, political, ideological and cultural construct. She writes that "woman' has meaning only in heterosexual systems of thought and heterosexual economic systems'.[4]

The discussion of women's art and women artists is, many feminists feel, crucial to feminism. After all, *we know what male artists are like,* and we are utterly familiar with male art. We are surrounded, embedded, drenched, choked, and smothered by patriarchal art and culture, by male-orientated – even if not specifically male-*made* – culture. Male projections, often onto women, have become dogma. Masculinist fears of the body, and sexuality, have been projected onto women, so that the vagina becomes a hell hole, the 'gateway to Hell'. As Luce Irigaray writes: men's '*fantasies lay down the law*'.[5] In a patriarchal culture, male art is seen as the hegemony which (female) feminists have to subvert. For too long, some feminists claim, women's art has been defined as simply 'not male'/ 'men's art'. It is defined by its non-inclusion in the traditional sphere of men's/ male/ masculinist art. As Irigaray puts it: '[b]eing a woman is equated with not being a man.' (Je, 71)

There are many feminists who advocate the exaltation of all manner of women artists, who argue for a women's art based on women artists, who want us to look at women artists. There are other feminists who deny the primacy of the author, who say that the work – the text – is primary, who deny the transparency of the text (this is one of Julia Kristeva's projects).

Toril Moi and many other feminist critics have questioned the humanist notion of 'realism' or 'authenticity', where a text is seen to reflect the actual experience of the one who created it. Humanist criticism sees a direct relation between author and text, assuming that the artwork is a direct expression of the artist's experience. Artists, however, know that very often the artwork ends up being far away from what they intended to express or communicate. Texts do not simply reflect directly the author's perception of life. The only assessment of a text would be how well the author has perceived the 'real world'. These approaches ignore how complex textual production is, with its many literary and non-literary influences, including the social, political, institutional and psychological (T. Moi, 1985, 45). 'It is in the significant *silences* of a text, in its gaps and absences that the presence of ideology can be most positively felt', writes Terry Eagleton.[5]

Hélène Cixous says, in the famous article "The Laugh of the Medusa", '[a]nd why don't you write? Write! Writing is for you, you are for you… Write, let no one hold you back, let nothing stop you' (M, 246-7). For Cixous (who is loved and loathed by feminists nearly as energetically as Andrea Dworkin or Camille Paglia or Princess Diana), writing is absolutely crucial, and central; it is oxygen to her, she must write to live, as she says:

> Having never been without writing, having writing in my body, at my throat, on my lips… to me my texts are elements of a whole which inter-weaves my own story. ("Preface", C, xv)

You can 'read' creatively, if you don't write. Much of feminist theory is based on 'reading' texts as a woman, a feminist, a lesbian. If the author is 'dead', and the text is primary, then deeply engaging with texts is crucial. Hence the importance, too, of feminist æsthetic and philosophic criticism, which aims to interpret all manner of texts. The reader, at least, is 'real'. The reader, it would seem, is truly flesh and blood, not a linguistic abstraction. Even here, though, some feminists dispute the 'reality' or 'authenticity' of the body, for the body, like education or desire or the family, is culturally and socially conditioned. That is, there is no such thing as a 'pure' reality, a 'pure' experience, a 'pure' response to a text, a response that is not modulated by all manner of societal, familial, psychological, political, ideological and cultural influences. In feminism, the scenario is not simply a woman and a book, existing completely separately from everything else, in some utopian place. No, there is so much that gets in the way of the seemingly 'innocent' or 'pure' exchange between a woman and an artwork, a person and a text. But the personal response is crucial, and alive. Reading can be, in itself, radical and transformative.

For Elizabeth Grosz, the body isn't simply a natural or organic thing or process; there is always a lot more going on with the body – to do with the cultural, social and psychological impact on it, as she explains in her stunning book *Volatile Bodies*:

> What psychoanalytic theory makes clear is that the body is literally written on, inscribed, by desire and signification, at the anatomical, physiological, and neurological levels. The body is in no sense naturally or innately psychical, sexual, or sexed. It is indeterminate and indeterminable outside its social constitution as a body of a particular type. This implies that the body which it presumes and helps to explain is an open-ended, pliable set of significations, capable of being rewritten, reconstituted, in quite other terms than those which mark it, and consequently capable of reinscribing the forms of sexed identity and psychical subjectivity at work today. (60-61)

As Elizabeth Grosz reminds us, human beings always live in their bodies: they always have a body. They can't remain human without a body:

> Human subjects never simply *have* a body; rather, the body is always necessarily the object and subject of attitudes and judgements. It is psychically invested, never a matter of indifference. Human beings love their bodies (or, what amounts libidinally to the same thing, they hate them or parts of them). The body never has merely instrumental or utilitarian value for the subject. (ib., 81)

Even when it is nude, the body exhibits traces of its culture, its society, its politics, its use, and its practices, as Grosz notes:

> The naked European/ American/ African/ Asian/ Australian body (and clearly even within these categories there is enormous cultural variation) is still marked by its disciplinary history, by its habitual patterns of movement, by the corporeal commitments it has undertaken in day-to-day life. It is in no sense a natural body, for it is as culturally, racially, sexually, possibly even as class distinctive, as it would be it if were clothed.

In the advanced capitalist, technological world, the body is not a 'natural' form any more, as Elizabeth Grosz explains in *Volatile Bodies*: clothing, exercise, jewellery, lifestyle, habits, negotiations of the cultural and social as well as the physical environment, and all sorts of activities, alter it, inscribe it, turn it into something definitely not 'natural':

> Makeup, stilettos, bras, hair sprays, clothing, underclothing mark women's bodies, whether black or white, in ways in which hair styles, professional training, personal grooming, gait, posture, body building, and sports may mark men's. There is nothing natural or ahistorical about these modes of corporeal inscriptions. Through them, bodies are made amenable to the prevailing exigencies of power. They make the flesh into a particular type of body – pagan, primitive, medieval, capitalist, Italian, American, Australian. (142)

LUCE IRIGARAY'S POETICS

Luce Irigaray concentrates on the act of enunciation, the act of producing discourse. Irigaray stresses the interiority of the speaking subject, the traces of subjectivity found in acts of communication. The continual denial of a sexualized discourse threatens the possibility of an emergent non-patriarchal society. In *Thinking the Difference* she wrote:

> When women use *je* as the subject of a sentence, this woman *je* most often addresses a man and not another woman or women. It does not relate to itself either. (46)

Luce Irigaray has investigated the use by men and women of everyday language, concluding that men and women privilege different patterns of speech, with men encouraging their 'self-affection', or relations to/ with the self and the self projecting in others, while women use language to make connections and relationships with both sexes. Irigaray's decon-struction of the languages of science, philosophy and politics has demon-strated the repression of the feminine – Dale Spender and other feminists have come to similar conclusions. For Irigaray, this repression is not built into language, but reflects the (patriarchal) social order. What women may signify in patriarchal or masculinist culture is an excess which points towards 'something else', demonstrating that masculine culture is not everything, does not have a monopoly on appropriation or value (Sex, 74f).

Language is central to the creation of a 'feminist æsthetics'. Women are denied the place to really *speak*, as many feminists note. Luce Irigaray writes in "The poverty of psychoanalysis":

> When a girl begins to talk, she is already unable to speak of/to herself. Being exiled in man's speech, she is already unable to auto-affect. Man's language separates her from her mother and from other women, and she speaks it without speaking in it. (I, 101)

For Luce Irigaray, 'rights for women' must include authentic self-images and self-representations of women: that is, an authentic, non-patriarchal women's art. In "How to define sexuate rights?" Irigaray writes that 'the right to human dignity' must include '[v]alid self-representations of women, in gestures, in words and images, in all public places' (1991, 208). For some feminists, the question of feminism is largely the question of representation, and perhaps the commonest complaint of feminists about the global is the poor quality and frequency of authentic self-representations of women. It is a problem broadcasters and magazine editors address from time to time, but, outside of a very few areas, the media in general is thoroughly patriarchal.

When Luce Irigaray writes on the media, she voices complaints about the masculinist bias of broadcasting that have been made before. They are complaints, however, worth making repeatedly:

> ...the choice of leisure activities available, and more specifically the media, feed into a between-men culture. Male sport is all-pervasive, and television stations don't hesitate in replacing a cultural programme aimed at both sexes with a football match. Women, however, pay the same as men to enjoy television programmes...

Women, as Luce Irigaray writes, 'are not the target audience'. But, even if they are the target audience of some shows (*Charmed, Sex and the City, Oprah,* etc), the actual shows themselves are patriarchal texts that carry patriarchal attitudes, values, images and morals. Irigaray writes:

> Male fantasies, on the other hand, find daily fulfilment in military, pornographic, and violent films that are of absolutely no interest to women.

Yet women pay for the television licence fee (in parts of Europe), as Luce Irigaray says:

> Media broadcasts, such as television, for which women pay the same taxes as men, [should] be half of the time targeted towards women. (Je, 89)

LUCE IRIGARAY, FRENCH FEMINISM
AND FRIEDRICH NIETZSCHE

Friedrich Nietzsche (1844-1900) has been one of the major philosophic encounters in the work of Luce Irigaray, and to a lesser extent in the work of Hélène Cixous and Julia Kristeva. Recent feminist analyses of Nietzsche have gone far beyond the stereotype of Nietzsche as a misogynist: his relation to the 'feminine', to 'woman' and 'women', is much more complicated than mere woman-hating and sexism.[8]

Every intellectual and writer seems to have to grapple with Friedrich Nietzsche as some time or other (especially the French philosophers: Georges Bataille, Hélène Cixous, Sarah Kofman, Gilles Deleuze, Jacques Derrida, and Jean-Paul Sartre). For Derrida in *Spurs*, Nietzsche's relationship with the feminine was embodied by his identification with three types of women: the castrating woman, the castrated woman, and the affirming woman. 'Nietzsche was all these', wrote Derrida – sometimes at once, successively or simultaneously.[10] For some feminist critics, the figure behind these masks may be Nietzsche's mother, and his ambiguous relationship with his mother may inform some of his ambivalent attitudes towards women.[11]

The influence of Lou Andreas-Salomé (1861-1937) on Friedrich Nietzsche has been noted by some feminist critics, including French feminist Sarah Kofman. Nietzsche was besotted with Andreas-Salomé, calling her 'sharp-sighted as an eagle and courageous as a lion'.[12] Andreas-Salomé was the only erotic/ philosophic focus in Nietzsche's otherwise celibate experience of women.[13] Kofman has wondered whether Andreas-Salomé was a model for that narcissistic woman which men love, the type that demands to be loved. Kofman considers this narcissistic woman in relation to Nietzsche, and wonders whether Andreas-Salomé was the mediator of the theory of narcissism between Nietzsche and Sigmund Freud.[13] Andreas-Salomé's notion of the narcissistic woman, and her thoughts on the artist, influenced Nietzsche.

In the Nietzschean-Andreas-Saloméan view, the (male) artist, if he is lucky, can aspire to the creativity of the woman, to become a 'birther' (*Gebärerin*), which may make him 'more whole, more organic, fused... with what he creates, just as woman is,' Andreas-Salomé wrote in her 1899 essay "Die in such ruhende Frau": 'and maintains him as it were in a joy of spiritual pregnancy, which lives deep within itself.'[14] Luce Irigaray was sceptical of such a project. Other critics have analyzed Hélène Cixous' reading of Nietzsche.[15]

✤

One of Luce Irigaray's main philosophic encounters has been with Friedrich Nietzsche. Irigaray's rewriting of Nietzsche, *Amante marine: De Friedrich Nietzsche*, has itself been the subject of much critical attention. The title itself is complex, being interpreted by critics as:

(1) a book about or by or in the person of the marine lover of Nietzsche, or

(2) 'the marine lover (or betrothed), a book on (de) Friedrich Nietzsche', or (3) the marine lover, a book by Nietzsche.[19]

Luce Irigaray takes on, in "Speaking of Immemorial Waters" (the first of three parts), the Nietzsche of *Thus Spoke Zarathustra*; in the second part, "Veiled Lips", Irigaray considers Nietzsche's concept of *such geben als, se donner pour*, the self-giving of woman and truth; the third section, "When Gods Are Born", tackles the deities Apollo, Dionysus and Christ. Irigaray's treatment of Nietzsche, however, is not straightforward, but multi-layered, ironic and lyrical. She writes not in a purely essay, lecture, novelistic or philosophical form.

The problem of the 'feminine' and 'feminism' in Friedrich Nietzsche's philosophy, which Luce Irigaray, Hélène Cixous and other feminists have analyzed, is a complex one. 'Perhaps I am the first psychologist of the eternally feminine', Nietzsche wonders in *Ecce Homo*.[20] For some feminist critics, though, Nietzsche's texts cannot be rescued from their sexist views on women and gender.[21] The Nietzschean project of the self-giving woman, the spiritually pregnant woman, forms a model for the (male) 'birther', an artist, who will become a 'birther', if he is lucky enough. Nietzsche saw in 'spiritual pregnancy' a way into the contemplative

personality type, or the 'male mother'.[22] Irigaray does agree with Nietzsche on the subject of 'spiritual pregnancy' in "Ecce Mulier":

> Assurément la fécondité spirituelle existe. Elle a lieu parfois en deça ou
> au-déla de tout discours. [Certainly spiritual fecundity exists. It some-
> times occurs before or beyond all discourse] (EM, 318-9)

For Luce Irigaray, Friedrich Nietzsche's project of creativity via
'woman' is doomed to fail: '[y]ou will never have pleasure in woman, if
you insist on being woman.' (ML, 39) For Irigaray, Nietzsche's notion of
self-seduction or 'self-marriage' is a failure, because it does not acknow-
ledge the woman, the important psychic relationship of 'you in her, and
her in you' (ML, 73).

❧

Julia Kristeva's relation to Friedrich Nietzsche has been less important
than in the work of Hélène Cixous and Luce Irigaray. Jacques Lacan and
Sigmund Freud figure much larger in Kristeva's theory than Nietzsche.
Kristeva is sceptical of Nietzsche's philosophy in *About Chinese Women*,
when she writes: 'Nietzsche would not have known how to be a woman. A
woman has nothing to laugh about when the symbolic order collapses.'
(K, 150) Even so, some critics have seen similarities between the
philosophies of Kristeva and Nietzsche, between the notion of rebirth (in
Kristeva's interpretation of melancholy and Nietzsche's revaluation of
values).[16] Nietzsche's relation to the maternal is more in tune with
Kristeva's poetics. Nietzsche's problem was that he conflated 'woman',
the 'feminine' and motherhood: in his works, woman becomes 'the fetish
of eternal pregnancy', a phallic mother of eternal potency: sexually, she is
feared, but as a mother she is exalted.[17] For Sigmund Freud, the fetish was
a substitute for the missing penis of the mother, a view that perpetuated
the fantasy of the phallic mother; Nietzsche fetishized the womb and
women's (spiritual) fecundity. He spoke in Goddess-oriented terms, the
kind familiar from thousands of years of mythology and poetry, of the
'eternally creative primordial mother'.[18] In "Fetishization", Elizabeth
Grosz is illuminatingly clear:

The fetishist demands, in spite of recognizing its impossibility, that there be a maternal phallus. He simultaneously affirms and denies that the mother is castrated... Fetishization renders the object into an image of another, genital object, thereby sexualizing it and making it into an appropriate or worthy object of desire for the subject. It thus describes a common male mode of objectification of women's bodies. (1992, 117)

LUCE IRIGARAY AND JACQUES LACAN

For French feminists such as Hélène Cixous, Jacques Lacan's (1901-81) philosophy of the Lacanian 'lack' is ridiculous. As she writes in "The Laugh of the Medusa": '[w]hat's a desire originating from a lack? A pretty meagre desire.' (M, 262) And Luce Irigaray and other feminists (Sarah Kofman, Elizabeth Grosz, Michèle Montrelay and Mary Ann Doane) have criticized the Freudian-Lacanian emphasis on the phallus as the 'transcendental signifier', as the measure of authentic sexual pleasure.[24] What woman lacks is lack itself, says Montrelay, an inability to create distance and representation.

From Plato to Sigmund Freud and Jacques Lacan, the desire and lack has been central to Western sexual metaphysics: in this negative model, one is doomed to a desire for more and more consumption, which leads to dissatisfaction. Freudian-Lacanian desire can never be satisfied: dissatisfaction is built-in. Desire is never annihilated: for Georg Wilhelm Friedrich Hegel, only another desire can satisfy desire and also perpetuate it. Desire thus desires more desire (this has a vivid expression in late capitalist consumerism, where it is always the *next* commodity that will truly satisfy and stop the hunger for more objects. But it never happens).

Far better to see desire, as Elizabeth Grosz does, as a positive force, one which (following Baruch Spinoza and Friedrich Nietzsche as opposed to Georg Wilhelm Friedrich Hegel and Sigmund Freud), makes connections and alliances. Instead of regarding desire as a repetitive search for something to make up for a central, gaping loss, it is seen as a force of production and creative assemblage; not fantasmatic but real.[25] This view of desire (in the work of Nietzsche, Spinoza, Gilles Deleuze and Félix Guattari), is also that of Hélène Cixous and Luce Irigaray (Julia Kristeva seems to be less convinced, and more committed to a post-Lacanian reading of desire). Desire becomes not yearning but actualization, actions, creation: instead of a Lacanian lack, desire becomes primary. As Cixous says: 'my desires have invented new desires' (M, 246).

The Lacanian Look emphasizes eroticism. Seeing is erotic, the eye becomes a kind of phallus, caressing the obscure object of desire, which it can never 'possess'. As the poet Rainer Maria Rilke wrote: '[g]azing is a wonderful thing.'[26] The act of looking eroticizes the object. Jack Zipes explains:

> For [Lacan], seeing is desire, and the eye functions as a kind of phallus. However, the eye cannot clearly see its object of desire, and in the case of male desire, the female object of desire is an illusion created by the male unconscious. Or, in other words, the male desire for woman expressed in the gaze is auto-erotic and involves the male's desire to have his own identity reconfirmed in a mirror image. (1986, 258)

The Look is an assertion of male power and sexuality. For the gaze is male, or masculine, and feminists have grappled with the notion of a female gaze.[27] 'Male desire is presented as a response to female beauty', writes Andrea Dworkin (*Intercourse*, 114). Margaret Whitford glosses Luce Irigaray's work in 1991 thus:

> Western systems of representation privilege *seeing*: what can be seen (presence) is privileged over what cannot be seen (absence) and guarantees Being, hence the privilege of the penis which is elevated to the status of the Phallus. (30)

Lacanian psychoanalysis is a hell of misrepresentations and mis-readings, mirrors and imaginary spaces. The subject in the Lacanian system is constantly trying to make good mistakes made in its early psychosexual growth. In the dreaded mirror phase, the image becomes a mirage, and a distance is set up between the image and the body, an absence which Jacques Lacan termed the *objet a*. In the confusions of the three realms, the symbolic, real and imaginary, the subject cannot realize what it most wants to realize. The objects of desire remain forever elusive.

There is something inexplicably depressing about Jacques Lacan's version of psychosexual events. Lovers, in the Lacanian system, desire what they cannot have. The problem of the lack, the *objet a* and *la chose*, can never be resolved. Lacanian philosophy posits, among other things (here we go again): an eternal search for what can never be found.[28] The Freudian-Lacanian system demands a continuous series of substitutions for objects to fill the primordial lack. It is a system of replacing an imaginary and immobile plenitude that will always fail. The primal realm remains always lost or forbidden. The Paradise of early childhood recedes ever further into the distance of the past.

Meanwhile, in the Jungian system, Beatrice, Laura, Cleopatra, Isolde, Eurydice, Ariadne and all those women of myth, poetry and legend, are incarnations of the *anima*, which is, as Carl Jung explains, something all males possess: '[e]very man carries with him the eternal image of woman, not the image of this or that particular woman, but a definitive feminine image.'[29] The *anima* is 'a personification of the unconscious in a man, which appears as a woman or a goddess in dreams, visions and creative fantasies', comment Emma Jung and Marie-Louise von Franz.[30] Male painters throughout history have depicted their version of the *anima*, it seems. Each (male) painter has a version of the 'inner feminine figure' as Jung calls her in *Memories, Dreams, Reflections* (210-1). For painters, this idealized *anima* figure seems to be another manifestation of that obscure object of desire, the eroticized woman, a mirror for male lust. The equation is: the more sublime and voluptuous the woman is painted, the more sublime and voluptuous is the artist's desire. The artist's model, then, can be seen as a Jungian *anima*, heavily eroticized, a Lacanian phallic mirror.

Further: in Lacanian psychology, desire, which is the foundation of the system, is enmeshed with speaking, with creativity and art. The œdipal crisis and the repression of the desire for the mother occurs with the entry into the Symbolic Order, and the entry into language. As Toril Moi crystallizes Jacques Lacan's ideas so concisely in *French Feminist Thought*: '[t]o speak as a subject is therefore the same as to represent the existence of repressed desire.' (99-100) The links between seeing and erotic pleasure, between the eye and the phallus, are found in much of Western 'high culture': not only in the history of painting, but also in the great works of poets such as Dante Alighieri, Francesco Petrarch, William Shakespeare and the troubadours. In the 'classic' text of pornography, Georges Bataille's *The Story of the Eye*, there are eyes placed in mouths, vulvas and anuses. Bataille takes the Sadeian ethic of the pornographic Look to its logical, literal extreme.[31]

Men gaze at women and manipulate them into erotic poses. Larysa Mykyta writes in 1983:

> The sexual triumph of the male passes through the eye, through the con-templation of the woman. Seeing the women ensures the satisfaction of wanting to be seen, of having one's desire recognized, and thus comes back to the original aim of the scopic drive. Woman is repressed as subject and desired as object in order to efface the gaze of the Other, the gaze that would destroy the illusion of reciprocity and oneness that the process of seeing usually supports. The female object does not look, does not have it own point of view; rather it is erected as an image of the phallus sustaining male desire.[32]

The pleasure of the text, whether the text is a painting, movie, magazine, photograph, piece of theatre, etc, comes, according to Roland Barthes, when the Look of the spectator is aligned with that of the author.[33] What feminist criticism has done is to question the masculine 'pleasure of the text', arguing for a feminist reading of the traditional masculine or patri-archal view of texts.

For some feminists, however, there can be no true 'feminist gaze', because the Look is always masculine, ultimately. If the spectator is a 'gendered object', suggests Annette Kuhn in *Women's Pictures: Feminism and the Cinema*, then 'masculine subjectivity [is] the only subjectivity available' (1982, 63). The politics of representation, which are central to the consumption of culture and art, are weighted firmly in favour of men and patriarchy. As John Berger remarked: 'men act and women appear'. And as Catherine King notes:

> most images in masculine visual ideology are created to empower men as spectators – that is, to see themselves as endlessly important with things laid out for their desire.33

Post-Lacanian feminists such as Luce Irigaray argue that subjectivity can only be attributed to women with difficulty. Irigaray claims that 'any theory of the subject has always been appropriated by the 'masculine'' (S, 133). 'Woman' is tied to a 'non-subjective subjectum' (S, 265). Irigaray stresses the sexed being, the sexualized subject and speaking position. No form of knowledge or philosophy can be authentic or 'universal' if it ignores the female position.

Luce Irigaray says that if the vagina is regarded as a 'hole', it is a 'negative' space that cannot be represented in the dominant discourse: thus to have a vagina is to be deprived of a voice, to be decentred or culturally subordinated, and so Irigaray replaces Jacques Lacan's mirror with a vaginal speculum.34 The phallic privileging of the masculine 'I' (penis, phallus, power, identity, soul), means that female sexuality is rendered 'invisible', just as the vagina is a negative space or void. The phallus is the divine, beloved mirror, emblem of masculine narcissism. But the vulva, being a 'black hole', can reflect back nothing. There is no self there. Male speculations and narcissistic gazes create a male subject. The Western philosopher's speculations are narcissistic. The mistakes arise when this male subject is equated with the whole world. The universality of philosophy and psychoanalysis thus becomes founded on a one-sided (male) view of the world. Male sexuality and narcissism mistakenly becomes the basis for the universal model of sexuality in psychoanalysis. Female sexuality becomes the negative image of male sexuality, the 'specularized Other',[36] if female subjectivity is considered at all. Women are supposed to have 'penis envy', a hankering for the transcendent signifier which will enable them to attain a positive, creative identity. Freudian 'penis envy' has been rejected by most feminists.

One can see how Luce Irigaray would have upset Jacques Lacan, who founded his theory of sexuality, like Sigmund Freud, on the primary of the phallus. In the Freudian-Lacanian phallic system, all is unity, identity, singularity (all the way back to that initial 'singularity', the Big Bang). Ambiguity, multiplicity and excess are excluded from this view: Irigaray's project of rewriting Freud and Lacan disrupts the isomorphic unity and replaces it with a series of dense, poetic, parodic discourses, in which female repression is unleashed and the female unconscious is allowed to explode into academic patriarchy.

Luce Irigaray's specular project disrupts the insistence in phallic, patri-archal sexuality on one organ (penis), one orgasm or pleasure (male), one identity (male), and one model of representation (masculine). Irigaray's notion of feminine writing disrupts the unitary dimensions of the phallo-cratic system ('there would be no longer either subject or object', Irigaray wrote of the new 'female syntax' in *This Sex Which Is Not One*, and "oneness' would no longer be privileged' [134]). 'You fail to recognize one simple *fact*: women can come without any help from you', Irigaray tells a group of imaginary psychoanalysts (I, 93).

For Madeleine Gagnon, the phallus is a symbol of political as well as psychological oppression for feminists: the phallus 'represents repressive capitalist ownership, the exploiting bourgeois, the higher knowledge that must be gotten over'. It means regimentation, representation, perfection (M, 180).

For some feminists, Luce Irigaray's rewriting of Jacques Lacan's work is still as essentialist as Lacan's phallic discourse; for others, Irigaray's speculum discourse is not essentialist, for 'Irigaray is nobody's fool, [and] not Lacan's'.[37] Some critics who are more sympathetic to Irigaray's thought (Margaret Whitford, Naomi Schor, Jane Gallop, Elizabeth Grosz, Josette Féral, Katherine Stephenson, Carolyn Burke, Diana Fuss) offer a more sophisticated reading than those feminist critics (Toril Moi, Monique Plaza, Janet Sayers, Ann Jones) who see nothing but essentialism in Irigaray's philosophy.[38] Plaza says Irigaray's method is *'completely under the influence of patriarchal ideology'* (1978, 31, my emphasis). Irigaray, though, emphasizes not so much biological as morphological feminist strategies: her emphasis is very much on forms of representation of the body, and how these modes of representation relate to society and social ethics. It is the social inscription of corporeality, not the anatomical body in itself, that is important.

3

✺

LUCE IRIGARAY, FRENCH FEMINISM, SEXUALITY, AND SEXUAL DIFFERENCE

When feminists discuss the body and sexuality, the results are just as controversial as their discussions of issues such as art vs. pornography, or the ways in which female power can be asserted in the social and political arena. Many feminists speak of the sexual superiority of women (compared to men, that is!), or, if not 'superiority', then at least a sexuality that is more sophisticated, more dangerous, more exhilarating, more subtle, and more sensual – well, that amounts to 'superior'. For instance, Xavière Gauthier, a contemporary of Hélène Cixous, Luce Irigaray and Julia Kristeva, says that:

...witches [women] are bursting; their entire bodies are desire; their
gestures are caresses; their smell, taste, hearing are all sensual. Their
pleasure is so violent, so transgressive, so open, so fatal, that men have
not yet recovered... Female eroticism is terrifying; it is an earthquake, a
volcanic eruption, a tidal wave. It is disquieting and so is mystified. It is
made a mystery.[1]

This transgressive, terrifying eroticism has not yet really been depicted
in art or pornography for feminists. What we get is men's version of it –
male ideas of wild eroticism, with violence as a recurring ingredient.
Hélène Cixous reckons that women have an 'infinite', 'cosmic' libido, an
eroticism which is always in flux, and so minute and subtle, it goes far
beyond male/ masculine sexuality.

Almost everything is yet to be written by women about femininity:
about their sexuality, that is, its infinite and mobile complexity, about
their eroticization, sudden turn-ons of a certain miniscule-immense
area of their bodies; not about destiny, but about the adventure of such
and such a drive, about trips, crossings, trudges, abrupt and gradual
awakenings, discoveries of a zone at one time timorous and soon to be
forthright. A woman's body, with its thousand and one thresholds of
ardor... (M, 256)

Women have an all-over, total body eroticism, say writers such as
Anaïs Nin, Peter Redgrove and Luce Irigaray (and so do some men!). 'But
woman has sex organs just about everywhere. She experiences pleasure
almost everywhere', asserts Irigaray (yes, but so do many men!).[2]
Feminists have spoken of the wildness of women's eroticism and their
fantasies. What this stance does is to uphold the eternal philosophical
dualism of the West, setting women always against men, and using men
to gauge women's sexuality. Feminists such as Hélène Cixous have
argued, rightly, that masculine 'binary logic', which constantly opposes
terms such as 'masculine' and 'feminine', is very limiting. It is two-term
logocentrism, which reduces everything to 'yes' or 'no' (NBW, 63f).

Pornography, like art, pivots around *desire*. And desire, as Hélène
Cixous notes, is something that never dies: '[d]esire never dies', she says

LUCE IRIGARAY

(NBW). Cixous asks in *The Newly Born Woman*:

> How do I experience my sexual pleasure?… What is feminine *jouissance*, where is it sited, how is it inscribed in her body, in her unconscious? And then, how can it be written? (NBW, 151)

The problem is that *jouissance* operates outside of culture or language: but, to use *jouissance*, to wield its power, some critics claim, one has to incorporate it somehow into language and expression. The radical otherness of *jouissance* becomes distorted and circumscribed if it continues to remain outside of language, or in the body (C. Duchen, 98).

Julia Kristeva writes in *About Chinese Women* that:

> no other civilization seems to have made the principle of sexual differ-ence so crystal clear: between the two sexes a cleavage or abyss opens up… Monotheistic unity is sustained by a radical separation of the sexes: indeed, it is this very separation which is its prerequisite. (K, 141)

✤

One of the most fiercely contended areas of feminism, gay, lesbian, and queer theory, women's studies, and gender studies (whatever one wants to call it), is the issue of sexuality, and how it relates to gender, identity, art, pornography, representation, ideology, and politics. In the realm of feminism and gender/ gay/ lesbian/ queer sexuality studies, there is no single narrative thread to follow, but a bewilderingly intricate web of strands, layers, spaces and realms. The brief discussion that follows of sexual difference/ sexuality/ identity/ gender issues will not proceed in a satisfyingly logical and A to B fashion, but in a circular, perhaps spiral, certainly a squiggly way. In gender/ gay/ lesbian/ queer/ sexuality/ women's studies, what we find are the commentators, feminists and writers revolving and rehearsing and gassing about the same issues, time after time.

Luce Irigaray in her famous description of women's sexuality says women have an all-over eroticism, a total body sensuality, where the whole of the skin is alive to touches. 'The whole of my body is sexuate. My sexuality isn't restricted to my sex and to the sexual act (in the narrow sense)', asserts Irigaray (Je, 53). In *Parler n'est jamais neutre* Irigaray wrote: '[a]ll women can do is return to some tactile infinite/ unfinished. Touch, the substratum of all the senses, acts before any clear-cut positioning of subject and object' (I, 108). For some feminists, Irigaray's morphology of female creativity is empowering, 'a challenge to the traditional construction of feminine morphology where the bodies of women are seen as receptacles for masculine completeness.' (Moira Gatens)³ Other feminists see the emphasis on just one form of female sexuality as a distinctly reductive and inauthentic kind of feminism:

> If we define female subjectivity through universal biological/ libidinal givens [writes Ann Rosalind Jones], what happens to the project of changing the world in feminist directions? Further, is women's sexuality so monolithic that shared, typical femininity does justice to it? What about variations in class, in race, and in culture among women? about changes over time in *one* woman's sexuality? (with men, with women, by herself?) How can one libidinal voice – or the two vulval lips so startlingly presented by Irigaray – speak for all women?⁴

Some feminists (such as Anaïs Nin) argue for multiple sexualities, for a plurality of sexualities, as against the standard, traditional notions of heterosexuality, homosexuality, lesbianism and bisexuality. Some feminists argue for the use of erotic feeling as a political weapon. Instead of denying eroticism, some feminists propound an ethics of glorifying sexuality. The body then becomes the centre, the subject, instead of being merely the object of male lust. Eroticism then becomes a source of power, as Audre Lorde explains:

> The erotic is a resource within each of us that lies in a deeply female and spiritual plane, firmly rooted in the power of our unexpressed or unrecognized feeling.⁵

Women speak of their eroticism in fiction and fantasy as being multisensual, not simply a matter of the visual or haptic senses, but of every sense, and more, in a synæsthetic experience.

In those early mornings it all tasted of sex after a few moments... The whole room seemed full of our commingled, complicated smells. And over and over again I'd come, sometimes still nearly asleep

wrote Sue Miller in *The Good Mother*,[6] while Summer Brenner remarked: 'our bodies made light in a soft room'.[7] Susan Griffin has written powerfully of lesbian eroticism in *Viyella*:

> ...my most profound longings and desires, for intimacy, to know, to touch and be inside the body and soul of another, becoming and separating from, devouring and being devoured, that wild, large, amazing, frightening territory of lovemaking belongs for me not with men, but with women.[8]

Nancy Friday has collected women's fantasies in a number of books: *My Secret Garden, Women On Top* and *Forbidden Flowers*. The fantasies involve lesbianism, group sex, sex with animals, sex with pop and movie stars, rape, anal sex, domination, S/M and all manner of erotic activities. Women's fantasies, like their fictions, are, some feminists believe, wilder, larger, more amazing and more frightening, to use Susan Griffin's words, than male fantasies and fictions. The books of erotic fiction and fantasy by women demonstrate something of the erotic ecstasy of women which, as Xavière Gauthier writes, 'is so violent, so transgressive, so open, so fatal, that men have not yet recovered.'[10]

Luce Irigaray talks about the 'very openness' of women's bodies, 'of their flesh, of their genitals', so that boundaries become difficult to define (I, 112). Irigaray speaks of two kinds of erotic *jouissance* – the phallic kind of orgasm, which men are concerned with and brag about – and the *jouissance* in harmony with a female libidinal economy (I, 45). Irigaray's point is that there are forms of *jouissance* other than the phallocratic model. Incredible though women's sexual fantasies may be, they are always defined in terms of masculinist fantasies, often in terms of difference. Julia Kristeva's form of *jouissance* is not Jacques Lacan's phallic or sexual *jouissance*, but a *jouissance* that is ecstasy. For erotic pleasure, Kristeva uses the term *plaisir* (DL, 160).

LESBIAN, GAY AND QUEER THEORY;
MONIQUE WITTIG AND FRENCH FEMINISM

Some feminists regard sexuality as expressed through performances and gestures, rather than being some essence. Thus heterosexuality itself is not an unchanging institution, but may already be a 'constant parody of itself', as Judith Butler suggests in *Gender Trouble* (1990, 122). Heterosexuality, Butler reckons, is continually imitating itself, always miming its own performances in order to appear 'natural'. Catherine MacKinnon wrote: '[s]exuality is that social process which creates, organizes, expresses, and directs desire, creating the social beings we know as women and men, and their relations create society.'[11] Adrienne Rich, in her influential essay "Compulsory heterosexuality and lesbian existence" (1980), says that heterosexuality is not 'preferred' or chosen, but has to be 'imposed, managed, organized, propagandized, and maintained by force'; for Rich, 'violent structures' are required by patriarchal society in order to 'enforce women's total emotional, erotic loyalty and subservience to men'.

Lesbian, gay and queer cultural theory has continually addressed the problem of identity and gender. There are certain sexual and social 'positions' or 'categories' which are seen as 'outside' the (patriarchal) norms, which may have affinities with the female 'outsider' figures of Julia Kristeva and Luce Irigaray. The lesbian, for instance, is sometimes seen as an 'outsider', like the black woman, or the feminist. Gender and sexual identity categories are becoming increasingly blurred.

For example, there are
- 'physical' lesbians,
- 'natural' lesbians,
- 'cultural' or 'social' lesbians,
- 'male' lesbians (men who position themselves as lesbians),
- men with vaginas and women with penises,
- there are queer butches and aggressive femmes,
- there are F2Ms and lesbians who love men,

- queer queens and drag kings,
- daddy boys and dyke mummies,
- bull daggers,
- porno afro homos,
- transsexual Asians,
- butch bottoms,
- femme tops,
- women and lesbians who fuck men,
- women and lesbians who fuck *like* men,
- lesbians who dress up as men impersonating women,
- lesbians who dress up as straight men in order to pick up gay men,
- butches who dress in fem clothing to feel like a gay man dressing as a woman,
- femmes butched-out in male drag,
- and butches femmed-out in drag.

Sexual/ social identities are continually being blurred, redefined, performed, questioned. Terms such as 'straight' and 'gay', 'hetero' and 'homo'/ 'hommo', are no longer adequate for these multi-layered, postmodern sexual identities. We need multiple genders – millions of genders. Two or three just ain't enough! There are many sexualities – surely as many as there are people, and also more (some people have multiple sexualities).

In lesbian and queer theory there are debates about the penis and the phallus: should lesbian sex involve penetration, which merely mimes heterosexual intercourse and perhaps upholds patriarchal norms? Is the lesbian use of the dildo 'subversive' or a parody? Does lesbian S/M mock or emulate straight sex? Is the lesbian butch/ femme social category simplistic and stereotypical? Is lesbian sexuality truly 'outside' patriarchal/ masculinist sexuality?

These are the concerns also of Hélène Cixous, Luce Irigaray and Julia Kristeva – the project of an erotic otherness, of an outside space or wild zone for women, a sexuality undefined and unfettered by masculinist discourse. Cixous especially (in "The Laugh of the Medusa"), has argued for a transgressive, radical, political and passionate form of female sexuality, which will go beyond male sexuality. The project is for a female sexuality that will not be a duplicate of masculinist sexuality, that will go beyond male narcissism, doubling and self-recognition. In *Speculum of the Other Woman*, Irigaray describes 'woman' as 'off-stage, off-side, beyond representation, beyond self-hood' (22).

Monique Wittig (1935-2003) is another powerful French feminist whose works, like those of Hélène Cixous, Luce Irigaray and Julia Kristeva, have been influential and controversial in the field of feminist cultural debate. Wittig is sometimes grouped with Irigaray and Cixous and the project of *écriture féminine*, but Wittig's view of 'lesbian writing' is not about exalting female difference, for in 'lesbian writing' sex is eliminated as a category. Wittig's works (*Les Guerillères, L'Opoponax, The Lesbian Body,* "The Straight Mind", "One Is Not Born a Woman", and *Virigile, non, Brouillon pour un dictionaire des amantes*), seem to offer a radical view of lesbians. Wittig positions lesbians somewhat as Kristeva and Cixous position women: as societal outsiders. In "The Straight Mind", Wittig sees lesbians as becoming nomads and runaways, as well as becoming more establishment. For Wittig, lesbians are outsiders in the heteropatriarchal system: Wittig's oft-quoted statement runs thus:

> Lesbian is the only concept I know of which is beyond the categories of sex (woman and man), because the designated subject (lesbian) is *not* a woman, either economically, or politically, or ideologically. (1980, 53)

In *Le corps lesbien*, Monique Wittig transformed the (male/ masculinist) 'I' of Western love poetry into the split 'J/e', the aim being to 'lesbianize the symbols' (1985, 11), so that Orphea saves her Euridice, and Christ becomes 'Christa the much-crucified'. For some feminists, Wittig has created in 'J/e' 'the most powerful lesbian in literature' (Elaine Marks);[12] Wittig's lesbian writings have created a new 'lesbian narrative space';[13] with an 'epistemological shift' away from phallocentrism;[14] Wittig's lesbian writing has nullified the masculinist social position (D. Crowder, 127).

For other feminists, Monique Wittig's project is simply too utopian and impractical: it makes the leap from imagination to representation without considering the practical difficulties of the proto-separatist lesbian utopia. Critics such as Judith Butler (in her book *Gender Trouble*) have seen that Wittig assumes a nostalgic once-upon-a-time social unity, which did not exist, and has never existed. Rather than rewriting or radically challenging notions of gender and sexuality, Wittig's texts affirm heterosexual and homosexual norms (1990, 115, 121). Wittig's view of lesbian sexuality and art is problematic: its relations to heteropatriarchy in particular are ambiguous. Wittig's texts, though, despite the confusions, offer an exuberant and thought-provoking revision of the heterosexual establishment.

Monique Wittig's lesbian philosophy is radical, in that she claims that lesbians are outside of heterosexual culture, and therefore the term 'woman' does not apply to them. In *Questions Féministes* in 1980, Wittig published an article ("The Straight Mind") which claimed that 'lesbians are not women' (1992, 32).

This form of (theoretical) lesbian separatism provides both a powerful position from which to speak, and an undermining of 'female' or 'women's' power. Being outside the group of (heterosexual) women could mean that it is difficult to change the heteropatriarchal system. For some feminists, one must work *within* the system in order to change it (you must be part of the Symbolic Order. as Julia Kristeva would say). Being a radical non-'woman' lesbian in Monique Wittig's view may render revolutionary change difficult. Making heterosexuality and men the 'enemy' as a whole, either socially or theoretically, renders some modes of change difficult, or even impossible. Radical lesbian separatism may be a position of power, but it is fraught with theoretical (and social, political, and ideological) difficulties. Wittig does recognize the social angle of oppression ('[i]t is oppression that creates sex and not the contrary', she says [1992, 2]).

Some commentators have over-emphasized the sexual aspect of Monique Wittig's conception of heterosexuality. For example, Judith

Butler in *Gender Trouble* has viewed Wittig's system of the binary sexual divide as 'serving the reproductive aims of a compulsory heterosexuality' (1990, 19). For Wittig, however, there is more to heterosexual oppression than sexual desire. There are also the social institutions of marriage and labour. Wittig writes (in 1982):

> The category of sex is the product of a heterosexual society in which men appropriate for themselves the reproduction and production of women and also their physical persons by means of...the marriage contract. (1992, 6)

Monique Wittig challenges conventional forms of the 'feminine' and language by

> not only reveal[ing] the violence done to women (entering language) but also turns the violence back on to language – the body of the text, of the word – and the body in the text. (J. Still, 1993, 24)

Simone de Beauvoir remarked of liberation for women: 'the first thing is work. Then refuse marriage if possible' (M, 147). In Luce Irigaray's view, women, in the psychoanalytic (Freudian/ Lacanian) system, are objects or commodities that are exchanged between men (I, 131). Freudian œdipalization becomes in fact an economy of female trade between men. Irigaray's theory of sexual difference envisages men as purveying a symbolic order of a hom(m)osexual economy, where there are only men, or castrated men. Women exist only in relation to men.

The significance of desire in Luce Irigaray's reading of psychoanalytic sexual economy is not as a lack or focussed on particular objects (women), but a circuit of flows and paths, detours and dynamics. In this narciss-istic, phallocentric monopoly, women are not the endpoint but the means or carriers of male desire. As it's between men, this sexual economy is homosexual, governed by and for men. The lesbian is thus a double negative in this social and metaphysical system: as a woman, she is silenced and negated; as a lesbian she disappears completely from the masculinist system of exchange. The lesbian subverts the economy of trade which is founded on the phallus.

Luce Irigaray playfully, ironically and at times bitterly rewrites Sigmund Freud's work. In her reading of Freud's view of lesbianism, for example, Irigaray deconstructs it to show that it is a fetish figure. Freudian 'female homosexuality', according to Irigaray, is a 'hom(m)osexualized' person, the woman who has a male desire for the phallic mother.

For Luce Irigaray, Sigmund Freud's lesbian performs a masculine masquerade in order to hide the double lack which is 'projected on to the lesbian body by the anxious gaze of the male voyeur-theorist'.²⁶ For Irigaray, masculinist views of lesbianism cannot escape from their phallocentric vision. Thus, lesbian *jouissance* is denied, because phallocentric patriarchy cannot envisage erotic pleasure between women that is not mediated by or motivated by male desire. Male ideologies such as Freudian psychoanalysis do not allow for female autoeroticism or homoeroticism. (For example, the regular scenario in porn – a man watching two women make love).

WOMEN AS WITCHES, OUTSIDERS, POETS

In the Neoplatonic, Aristotlean, Renaissance view of the fine art establishment, there is good art and bad art, there is the art of 'taste', 'decency', 'refinement', 'purity' and 'civilization', and there is the vulgar, the uncouth, the disrespectful, the unornamental, the unlearned. In mediæval culture, there is Sacred and Profane Love, drawn from Plato's *Symposium*, and the Venus Vulgaris (Earthly Venus) and Venus Coelestis (Heavenly Venus). The Heavenly Venus is the one to aspire to, even though the Earthly Venus may be much more exciting. These dichotomies are found throughout art. There is the chaste, passive, motherly Virgin Mary and the sexual, active, lascivious Mary Magdalene.[15] There is good and evil. There is Heaven and Hell.

There is male and female.

Throughout the history of Western culture we come across the same dualities, in one form or another. The female is clearly on the 'left' side, on the wrong side of the 'right' way. Women are the 'second sex', 'second class citizens': Sherry Ortner points out that there is an opposition between culture and nature, and women are lower down in the male-made hierarchy:

> my thesis is that woman is being identified with – or, if you will, seems to be a symbol of – something that every culture devalues, something that every culture defines as being of a lower order of existence than itself'.[16]

Women are imprisoned, as Hélène Cixous notes, in masculine binary logic, which is the 'classical vision of sexual opposition between men and women', as Verena Conley writes in her book on Cixous (1984, 129). For Luce Irigaray, this duality is called 'the recto-verso structure that shores up common sense' (I, 127).

Feminists speak of experiences beyond male control: pregnancy, childbirth, female orgasm, and *jouissance*. Annie Leclerc, perhaps the most 'essentialist' of French feminists, wrote of the orgasmic pleasures (*jouissances*) of childbirth, menstruation and lactation in her *Parole de femme*.[17] Julia Kristeva remarked in *About Chinese Women*:

> If a woman cannot be part of the temporal symbolic order except by identifying with the father, it is clear that as soon as she shows any sign of that which, in herself, escapes such identification and acts differently, resembling the dream of the maternal body, she evolves into this 'truth' in question. It is thus that female specificity defines itself in patrilinear society: woman is a specialist in the unconscious, a witch, a bacchanalian, taking her jouissance in an anti-Apollonian, Dionysian orgy. (K, 154)

Like the poet, woman is a shaman, a witch, a magician, moving beyond the symbolic/ œdipal/ patriarchal order; 'the female is the initiatrix', wrote Alex Comfort (1979). This is a continuing theme in the writings of Julia Kristeva. In "The True-Real" ("Le vréel"), she asserted:

> We know... how logic and ontology have inscribed the question of *truth* within *judgement* (or sentence structure) and *being,* dismissing as *madness, mysticism or poetry* any attempt to articulate that impossible element which henceforth can only be designated by the Lacanian category of the *real*. After the flowering of mysticism, classical rationality, first by embracing Folly with Erasmus, and then by excluding it with Descartes, attempted to enunciate the real as truth by setting limits on Madness; modernity, on the other hand, opens up this enclosure in a search for other forms capable of transforming or rehabilitating the statues of *truth*. (K, 217)

Myra Jehlen wonders that, if there is no extra-patriarchal space, can there be a feminist, non-patriarchal discourse?[17] Feminists such as Elaine Showalter and Jeanne Roberts, taking their cue from Edwin Ardener,[18] propose that there is a female 'wild zone', as there is a male 'wild zone'. We know about men's version of wild zone eroticism, what Hélène Cixous calls 'glorious phallic monosexuality' (M, 254). Female 'otherness' is beyond patriarchal space, beyond patriarchal representations.[19] Showalter in "Feminist Criticism in the Wilderness" suggests that, in terms of space, the female 'wild zone' 'is literally no-man's land, a place forbidden to men', while as (an) experience, it refers to aspects of women's life unavailable to or outside of male experience; metaphysically, it may be a space quite outside of masculine consciousness (ib., 262).

❖

Jacques Lacan called his notion of body image 'imaginary anatomy', which Elizabeth Grosz has defined in *Volatile Bodies* thus:

> The imaginary anatomy is an internalized image or map of the meaning that the body has for the subject, for others in its social world, and for the symbolic order in its generality (that is, for a culture as a whole). This, Lacan claims, helps to explain the peculiar, nonorganic connections formed in hysteria and in such phenomena as the phantom limb. It is also helps to explain why there are distinct waves of particular

forms of hysteria (some even call them fashions), i.e., why hysteria
commonly exhibited forms of breathing difficulty (e.g., fainting, tussis
nervosa, breathlessness, etc) in the nineteenth century which, by
comparison today, have relatively disappeared (perhaps with the
exception of asthma and various "allergic" reactions) and yet why,
taking their place as the most "popular" forms of hysteria today, are
eating disorders, anorexia nervosa and bulimia in particular. (39-40)

Always Luce Irigaray has been concerned with the notion of 'woman'
as 'outsider', of the otherness and outsideness of women in a patriarchal
regime. The feminine, says Irigaray, 'had to be deciphered as forbidden'
(S, 20). In *Speculum of the Other Woman*, Irigaray describes 'woman' as
'off-stage, off-side, beyond representation, beyond self-hood' (22).
Irigaray depicts 'woman' as philosophy's 'other', so she is interested in
those women who have been 'outsiders' in history – the hysteric, the
witch, the mediæval mystic, those people who 'stand outside' culture,
using the techniques of ecstasy ('exstase', Irigaray spells it, 'ecstasy'
meaning 'stand outside' – *ex-stase*, from the Greek). Both Irigaray and
Julia Kristeva spoke of the special creative positionality of the mediæval
women mystics, who occupied the maternal liminal place of the mother,
where the object of devotion became less fixed, more open, less dogmatic,
more 'feminine'. The female mystic may be able to stand outside of
(patriarchal) scopic representation, by being ecstatic. 'All desire is
connected to madness', Irigaray asserted in *Sexes et parentés* (I, 35). The
ecstatic experience of mysticism appears to escape (masculine) specular-
ization, its voyeurism and rationality (T. Moi, 1985, 136). According to
Elizabeth Grosz in "Lesbian Fetishism?", women can disavow their own
castration (*contra* Sigmund Freud) through hysteria – women phallicizing
part of their bodies; the 'masculine complex' – women taking the phallus
as their love object, and narcissism – women turning their bodies into the
phallus (E. Grosz, 1991).

Another figure that Luce Irigaray uses as a model of a new poetics and
feminism is the angel. Angels, says Irigaray, are never immobile, never
dwell in one place; they open up the closed world of identity, history and
action; angels continually pass through the world, 'postponing every

deadline, revising every decision, undoing the very idea of repetition';
angels are messengers, who 'transgress all limits by their speed', they are
beyond reductionism; their 'touch – when they touch – resembles that of
gods'; angels are sexual, too, deeply erotic even:

> It is as if the angel were the figurative version of a sexual being not yet
> incarnate [Irigaray wrote in *Ethique de la différence sexuelle*). A light,
> divine gesture from flesh that has not yet blossomed into action. Always
> fallen or still awaiting the Second Coming. The fate of a love still
> divided between the here and the elsewhere. (I, 173-4)

It seems as if Luce Irigaray is smitten by angelism, much as Rainer
Maria Rilke and Arthur Rimbaud were before her. Hélène Cixous wrote in
"The Laugh of the Medusa" of women as outsiders or witches, living in
the unconscious or the wilderness, who must return

> from afar, from always: from "without", from the heath where witches
> are kept alive; from below, from "beyond" culture... (M, 247)

An outcast or witch, 'woman' may also exist within the traditional
economies and languages. In Hélène Cixous' terms, 'woman' must be the
darer, the one who 'goes and passes into infinity', the traveller who 'alone
wishes to know from within', even though she is eternally the outcast (M,
260).

Julia Kristeva and Luce Irigaray, among other French feminists, have
spoken of something in women or the feminine that is 'unrepresentable',
beyond art, beyond male culture. 'Woman' is always negative, always
outside the symbolic realm; 'woman' 'isn't this (can't be defined), it isn't
yet that (isn't yet here)', Claire Duchen noted in *Feminism in France From
May '68 to Mitterand* (85).

Women, for Luce Irigaray, are out of touch with themselves, 'women are
nowhere, touching everything, but never in touch with each other, lost in
the air, like ghosts'. In *Parler n'est jamais neutre*, Irigaray suggests that
women need to re-connect with 'the imaginary of their desires', so they
would be 'at home everywhere', always in movement, their *jouissance*

would be in motion, 'nomads knowing only the frontiers of their living bodies' (I, 91).

This notion of 'woman' as 'outsider' is aligned to Julia Kristeva's notion of the *sujet-en-procès* and the 'negativity' of the text, which Kristeva developed in early works such as *Séméiotikè, La Révolution du langage poetique* and *Polylogue*. In *About Chinese Women*, Kristeva writes of the woman as a witch, someone outside of patriarchal discourse, or at least, thrown to the edge, the border between the known and the otherness:

> A *jouissance* which breaks the symbolic chain, the taboo, the mastery. A *marginal discourse*, with regard to the science, religion and philosophy of the *polis* (witch, child, underdeveloped, not even a poet, at best his accomplice). (K, 154)

Sherry Ortner writes that 'woman is being identified with – or, if you will, seems to be a symbol of – something that every culture devalues'.[17] Ann Rosalind Jones describes Kristeva's notion of the 'outsider' culture of women, of women as 'witches', in "Writing the Body: L'Écriture féminine":

> Women, for Kristeva... speak and write as "hysterics," as outsiders to male-dominated discourse, for two reasons: 'the predominance in them of drives related to anality and childbirth, and their marginal position vis-à-vis masculine culture. Their semiotic style is likely to involve repetitive, spasmodic separations from the dominating discourse, which, more often, they are forced to imitate.[20]

For Alice Jardine, Julia Kristeva's notion of the Other or alterity always ends up with the other sex. The first Other may be the mother, but Kristeva, Jardine maintains, 'has repeatedly pointed out that the Other is always in fact the "other sex"', and in "Opaque Texts" Jardine quotes Kristeva in *Revolution in Poetic Language*: '[t]he difference between 'I' and 'you' turns out to be coextensive with the sexual difference' (1984, 326). Kristeva's female voice, though, Jardine asserts, is 'strangely subversive'.[21]

Julia Kristeva's writings may be the most coherent and incisive account of psycho-cultural 'otherness'. Victor Burgin in "Geometry and Abjection", describing Kristeva's philosophy, says that she positions

> the woman in society… in the patriarchal, as perpetually at the bound-ary, the borderline, the edge, the 'outer limit' – the place where order shades into chaos, light into darkness. The peripheral and ambivalent position allocated to woman, says Kristeva, had led to that familiar division of the field of representation in which women are viewed as either saintly or demonic – according to whether they are seen as bring-ing the darkness, or as keeping it out.22

Saintly woman (the Virgin Mary is a typical example) keeps the amaz-ing energy of female otherness out of men's lives; the demonic woman (Mary Magdalene, the *femme fatale*, vampire, 'devil woman') is the one who brings the wildness with her. Patriarchy of course prefers bland, mute, passive door-stops in women, people who will stop the darkness from coming in, who will sit there and say nothing and get on with society's housework. Luce Irigaray's 'new woman' is someone eternally dissatisfied, always in the process of becoming, 'without end', without a model, someone who must cultivate, in the Nietzschean fashion of being a 'birther': she must:

> beget anew the maternal within her, give birth within herself to mother and daughter in a never-completed progression. She who possesses, in the darkness, the subterranean resource is mother; she who moves on the surface of the earth, in the broad light of day, is daughter. She becomes woman if she can unite within her the most secret energies that lie deepest in her body-womb, with life in the broad light of day. (I, 109)

André Breton said the 'existence is elsewhere'. French feminists say that 'woman' is elsewhere. 'She is indefinitely other in herself,' comments Luce Irigaray, maintaining that women

> are already elsewhere than in the discursive machinery where you claim to take them by surprise. They have turned back within them-selves, which does not mean the same thing as 'within yourself'. They do not experience the same interiority that you do and which perhaps

you mistakenly presume they share. (Sex, 68-69)

Here, perhaps, is female 'otherness', where some of the wildness and strangeness and ecstasy of female eroticism may be experienced and depicted. Luce Irigaray also spoke in spatial terms of idealist feminism in "La différence sexuelle":

> We need both space and time. And perhaps we are living in an age when *time must re-deploy space*. Could this be the dawning of a new world? Immanence and transcendence are being recast, notably by that *threshold* which has never been examined in itself: the female sex. It is a threshold unto *mucosity*. Beyond the classic opposites of love and hate, liquid and ice lies this perpetually *half-open* threshold, consisting of *lips* that are strangers to dichotomy. Pressed against one another, but without any possibility of suture, at least of a real kind, they do not absorb the world either into themselves or through themselves, pro-vided they are not abused or reduced to a mere consummating or con-suming structure. Instead their shape welcomes without assimilating or reducing or devouring. A sort of door unto voluptuousness, then? Not that, either: their useful function is to designate a *place*: the very place of uses, at least on a habitual plane. Strictly speaking, they serve neither conception nor *jouissance*. Is this, then, the mystery of female identity, of its self-contemplation, of that strange word of silence; both the thresh-old and reception of exchange, the sealed-up secret of wisdom, belief and faith in every truth?[24]

Many feminists suggest that women's eroticism cannot be represented, much as women themselves cannot be represented. Julia Kristeva writes: '[i]n "woman" I see something that cannot be represented, something that is not said, something above and beyond nomenclatures and ideologies.'[25] Other feminists echo this idea, that women cannot be fully represented in the traditional media of patriarchy. As Hélène Cixous says:

> It is at the level of sexual pleasure in my opinion that the difference makes itself most clearly apparent in as far as woman's libidinal economy is neither identifiable by a man nor referrable to the masculine economy. ("Sorties", M, 95)

The unrepresentable in art and pornography, according to some feminists, is women's eroticism, their *jouissance*, that 'explosive, blossoming, sane and inexhaustible *jouissance* of the woman', as Julia Kristeva describes it in *About Chinese Women* (63).

What we get in most Western art, from Greek and Roman sculpture through the glories of the Renaissance to the latest pornography, are male representations of female eroticism. Feminists say that there are no real depictions of female *jouissance* in art or literature. 'In my opinion,' remarked Marguerite Duras, 'women have never expressed themselves.'[26] What she means, perhaps, is that women have expressed themselves thus far in the terms and means defined by men. There is no 'feminine' or 'women's' writing, according to some feminists. For Duras, 'the future belongs to women. Men have been completely dethroned' (M, 238).

✤

Real sex, the French feminists argue, has not yet been represented. Women haven't done it because they work within the same patriarchal structures, codes and constraints as men. Men, generally, haven't got a hope of depicting authentic female eroticism, although the authors of millions of pornographic products would claim they know everything about female eroticism. On the other hand, in the mechanisms of cultural and postmodern theory, anyone, male or female, should be able to create a truly 'feminine' text. It shouldn't matter who the author is. If the French feminists are right, then nearly all of the art produced anywhere is oriented to the male and the masculine, *even* when it is created by *women*. Many women artists would dispute this. The notion of an 'authentic' 'women's'/ 'feminine' art continues to be hotly debated.[27]

Écriture feminine is a subversive position and activity, which deconstructs patriarchal (phallogocentric) language.[28] The 'sophisticated theoretical dilemma' of Hélène Cixous' was whether a 'female' or 'feminine' voice could be envisaged without 'acquiring its own kind of phallocentricity' (J. Duran, 174). If the woman's voice became phallocentric it was as if she had picked up the phallus itself. The fluid, plural and diffuse sense of 'feminine writing' subverts masculine culture.[29] Luce Irigaray privileges a poetry of women's laughter in the face of phallocracy; both Irigaray and Cixous advocate intimate, personal, precious languages of imaginary spaces that exist outside of phallocracy (L. Kipnis, 207). According to the French feminists, 'women's' or 'feminine' or 'female' art is created in the gaps and silences of a text, but not in the intentional space of the artwork. Mary Jacobus explains in "Is There a Woman In This Text?":

> The French insistence on *écriture féminine* – on woman as a writing-effect instead of an origin – asserts not the sexuality of the text but the textuality of sex. Gender difference, produced, not innate, becomes a matter of the structuring of a genderless libido in and through patri-archal discourse. Language itself would at once repress multiplicity and heterogeneity – true difference – by the tyranny of hierarchical oppositions (man/woman) and simultaneously work to overthrow that tyranny by interrogating the limits of meaning. The 'feminine', in this scheme, is to be located in the gaps, the absences, the unsayable or unrepresentable of discourse and representation. (1982, 14, 1)

For some feminists, philosophies based on the body are problematic, because to look for some essential nature of 'woman', some essence based in biology, is dubious.[30] Indeed, Toril Moi say that 'to define 'woman' is necessarily to essentialize her.' (1988, 139) Jacques Derrida had written in *Spurs* that

> There is no such thing as the essence of woman because woman averts, she is averted of herself. Out of the depths, endless and unfathomable, she engulfs and distorts all vestige of essentiality, of identity, of prop-erty. (51)

What is 'woman', anyway? A 'writing-effect', for the feminist Alice Jardine, an element in culture or a text. For Julia Kristeva, 'woman' does not 'exist', because there is no 'essence', no 'essential' woman (S. Hekman, 148). For Kristeva, not only 'woman' and the subject is 'in process' (*sujet-en-procès*), but the body and sexuality as well. French feminism produces a feminist 'space' rather than a 'sex'; the position is a cultural one, not, as in Anglo-American feminism, a discourse based on the biological woman. It's important, as Monique Wittig notes in "One Is Not Born a Woman", to make a distinction between the different interpretations 'woman' and 'women':

> Our first task... is thoroughly to dissociate "woman" (the class within which we fight) and "woman," the myth. For "woman" does not exist for us; it is only an imaginary formation, while "women" is the duct of a social relationship.[31]

Elaine Showalter writes of the biologic and genderized views of feminism in "Feminist Criticism in the Wilderness":

> Organic or biological criticism is the most extreme statement of gender difference, of a text indelibly marked by the body: anatomy is textuality... Simply to invoke anatomy risks a return to the crude essentialism, the phallic and ovarian theories of art, that oppressed women in the past.[32]

Biology, though, is crucial; the body is crucial.[32] Hélène Cixous states: '[i]n censuring the body, one censures at the same time breathing and speech.' (NBW, 179) But feminists such as Elaine Showalter are wary of biologist or essentialist philosophies, especially those of French feminism (see also J. Sayers, 1986, 42; T. Moi, 1985, 110; H. Wenzel, 1981, 284; M. Plaza, 1978).

As Simone de Beauvoir put it, women are not born, they are made, meaning socially, culturally, politically, ideologically, psychologically, etc. For de Beauvoir, 'nature plays an infinitesimal role in the development of a human being': instead, it was socialization that made all of the difference; it was everything that happened after birth. Thus, women were neither superior nor inferior to men, there was no 'eternal feminine', and 'a woman has no special value because she is a woman. That would be the most retrograde "biologism", in total contradiction with everything I think' (M, 153). Women are not 'superior' to men for Luce Irigaray: 'why think in quantative terms? They are *different*' (I, 190).

For Suzanne Horer and Jeanne Socquet, there was no point in simply following what men have done. That would mean repeating the same mistakes:

> We must not follow in the footsteps men have imprinted on this earth. Why repeat the same errors with the same too obviously, catastrophic results? We do not believe in social revolutions that aim at "changing man". Such jolts shift problems without ever solving them in depth. (M, 243)

Hélène Cixous, though, rejected the idea of a 'general woman', or a single type of feminine sexuality (in "The Laugh of the Medusa"). She said there was no essence in femininity or masculinity, but that 'everything is language'.[33] In *The Newly Born Woman* Cixous and Catherine Clément stated that there is 'no 'nature' or 'essence' as such', but, instead,

> living structures that are caught and sometimes rigidly set within historico-cultural limits so mixed up with the scene of History that for a long time it has been impossible (and it is still very difficult) to think or even imagine an 'elsewhere'... (1986, 83)

Appealing to the body is not necessarily essentialist, as feminists have noted.[34]

PART TWO

LUCE IRIGARAY

4

❀

"KISS MY LIPS": LUCE IRIGARAY'S PHILOSOPHY OF SEXUAL DIFFERENCE

Some of the more controversial aspects of French feminism, and in particular the feminisms of Hélène Cixous and Luce Irigaray, and to a lesser extent Julia Kristeva, include the insistence on the body, on biology, and on the sexual organs. Irigaray's pronouncements, above all others in French feminism, seem to have angered other feminists most of all. Of the French feminists who have become prominent in feminism since the 1970s (Cixous, Kristeva, Catherine Clément, Monique Wittig, Michèle Le Doeuff), Irigaray is one of the most consistently provocative. Her books of the 1970s *Ce sexe qui c'en est pas un* and *Speculum de l'autre femme* have been influential. With Cixous, Irigaray was one of the most powerful of the contributors to the key French feminist text in English, *New French Feminisms* (1981).

Luce Irigaray's post-Freudian, post-Lacanian feminist philosophy was based, at first, on, among other things, the body, on genitals which are continually embracing each other. Irigaray spoke of a 'door unto volupt-uousness'. For Irigaray, a woman's sex is 'two lips which embrace continually', in which women are parthenogenic, and self-contained, not needing others to pleasure them, because 'they are pleasuring themselves – continually' (ib., 100). This is what some critics find 'most specifically "feminine"' about Irigaray's idea, that is, 'its fantasy of the two-in-one' (M. Jacobus, 1986, 78). In Irigaray's metaphysics of 'self-touching', the woman as a whole [*tout*] touches it/herself: the/a woman is infinite, unfinished, not ready or not wishing to close up (I, 59). Openness is emphasized. The/A woman is not one, nor two, nor whole, nor infinite, because 'woman is always already in a state of anamorphosis in which all figures blur' (I, 56). The/A woman is not (never is) this or that at any one time, she is always in a state of becoming (I, 55). In Luce Irigaray's view in *Speculum*, the *jouissance* of the/a woman is an ecstasy of becoming, in which

> what comes to pass in the *Jouissance* of woman is in excess of it. An
> indefinite overflowing in which many a becoming could be inscribed.
> The fullness of their to-come is glimpsed, announced, as possibles, but in
> an extension, a dilation, without determinable limits. (I, 55)

The use by Luce Irigaray of the metaphor of the speculum, the medical curved mirror used for inspecting the vagina, introduces circularity, open-endedness and ambiguity into masculinist, phallic discourse. The curved mirror blurs contours and boundaries, it disrupts the clear, single reflection of the phallic order. The speculum rewrites the social order. 'Everything, then, should be rethought in terms of volute(s), helix(es), diagonal(s), spiral(s), curl(s), turn(s), revolution(s), pirouette(s)', said Irigaray (I, 64). Irigaray's polemic always emphasizes movement and alterity: in *Speculum de l'autre femme* she increases the kinetic emphasis, adding to the discussion of spirals and pirouettes a description of fracturing, bursting, whirling faster and faster, until 'matter shatters and falls into (its) dust' (I, 64-65).

Elizabeth Grosz has related Irigaray's labial trope to Maurice Merleau-Ponty's concept of two lips:

> these two lips are not those lived and experienced by women as such, although his metaphor may be an attempt to reappropriate this carnal intimacy of female corporeality: his lips remain each with their own identity and place, one on the side of the seer, the other on the side of the visible; neither can touch itself through touching the other – the point of Irigaray's self-enfolding metaphor – for neither is able to dissolve its boundaries through its intimacy with the other. (1995, 106)

In Luce Irigaray's morphology of sexuality, which can be seen as simplistic and reductive as well as inspirational, much of women's sexual identity is situated in the genitals. At this generalized level, she does not differ much from Sigmund Freud. But Irigaray does not simply replace the penis with the vagina, or, to speak in gender theory terms, the phallus with the womb. No, because the vagina is part of the patriarchal silencing of women. This is what Irigaray thinks: the vagina/ vulva/ womb has been silenced, negated, decentred, written out of mainstream (i.e., patriarchal) culture. The penis is exalted as the emblem of awe, holiness and presence, while the vagina is all absence. In Irigaray's possibly biologist feminist schema, the vulva is a cultural hole or vacuum which cannot speak, while the phallus, the 'transcendent signifier', is all mouth and speech. Irigaray thus moves swiftly from a theory of biology to culture, but retains her biologist basis for her feminist stratagem.

Luce Irigaray speaks of the denigration of the womb and vagina, the patriarchal reduction of women to 'cunt', to use the terminology of feminist analyses of pornography – specifically Andrea Dworkin's, the 'devouring mouth, a cloaca or anal and urethral outfall, a phallic threat', Irigaray calls it [I, 41]). Irigaray counters the hatred of the womb/ vagina by exalting the labia. The sex lips are autoerotic, always touching, and do not need anything masculine (least of all the penis) for their pleasure.

Phallic hierarchy is subverted, and is replaced with processes of reciprocity and circularity. Classical economies are subverted, because openness cannot be (re)produced. Infinite exchange replaces the closed, finite economy. The labia do not have boundaries, or barriers between them, they are both open and closed: the labial imagery encourages a *parlerfemme* ('speaking woman'/ 'speaking as woman').

> But when lips kiss, openness is not the opposite of closure [Irigaray wrote in *Elemental Passions*]. Closed lips remain open. And their touching allows movement from inside to outside, from outside to in, with no fastening nor opening mouth to stop the exchange. (63)

'The *lips*? The open, the infinite/ unfinished, not the indefinite retreat from the impossible to live, but opening, there, now, continually. *Retouching*', as Irigaray put it in *Parler n'est jamais neutre* (I, 110). Why focus on the labia in particular, though? Irigaray's enshrinement of the labia is linked to her notions of mirroring, self-enclosure, women's identity, and so on. But this exaltation of this or that part of the body is silly, ultimately. Why not enshrine the hands, which can offer just as much sexual pleasure and sexual identity and mirroring and self-enclosure as labial lips covered in juice? And what about the tongue – not only the tongue which licks and sucks at the genitals, the anus, etc, but tongues which kiss kiss kiss? Surely the tongue and mouth is a source of a vast amount of sexual *jouissance*? So important is the mouth, that some people regard kissing as more intimate than coition. The penis may be firmly buried inside the vagina, but if the participants aren't kissing, some people think they're not being wholly intimate! Prostitutes speak of not wishing to kiss their clients because that intimate pleasure is reserved for their lovers.

In those models and diagrams in medical text books which show how important the different external parts of the body are to the brain, the mouth and hands are shown as huge. In her project of enshrining women's sexuality and sexual difference, then, Luce Irigaray might have done better by choosing the hands or the mouth instead of the labia. The hands, for a start, seem to do much more than the labia – they stroke, touch, squeeze, rub and feather the skin. But then, men too have hands and tongues and mouths: and Irigaray wanted to exalt something specifically 'female'.

Why did she ignore, then, the supreme organ of female *jouissance*, the clitoris? Some feminists have criticized French feminists' insistence on the womb and labia, their ignoring of the clitoris, the organ of 'pure pleasure' (J. Sayers, 131).[1] So delicious is the clitoris, some men have admitted to feeling jealous of women. The clitoris is indeed suppressed in patriarchal culture – the vagina is at least 'necessary' for the furtherance of the species, men might say, for humanity needs children. But the clit seems to be the organ of pure pleasure and nothing else. It seems to have no other function than orgasmic pleasure.

If you are going to choose any single organ in a feminist sexual ethics, it has to be the clitoris. Why stop at hands and mouths? We need blood to live, and lungs, and the brain, etc. And what about the economies of genetics, history, politics, ideology, fantasy, imagination, family, gender, sociology and religion? All these, and others, have more bearing on sexual identity than this or that part of the body. The more one founds a theory of sexuality or sexual difference on the body, the sillier it becomes.

Shoshana Felman has criticized Luce Irigaray's writings on 'women's' art and 'feminist' æsthetics and their relation to biology and morphology:

> Is [Irigaray] speaking *as* a woman, or *in the place of* the (silent) woman, *for* the woman, *in the name of* the woman? Is 'speaking as a woman' a fact determined by some biological *condition* or by a strategic, theoretical *position*, by anatomy or by culture? What if 'speaking as a woman' were not a simple 'natural' fact, could not be taken for granted?[2]

In the chapter from *Speculum of the Other Woman* entitled "L'Incontourable volume", Luce Irigaray evokes the fluidity of the feminine in the terms of mediæval humours or elements. For her, 'woman' is wet through, an 'undefined flow that dampens, wets, floods, conducts, electrifies the gap, makes it glow in its blazing embrace.' (I, 64) In the interview "Les Femmes-mères, ce sous-sol muet de l'order social",[3] Irigaray wonders whether the Freudian-œdipal scenario (man/ god/ father killing the mother in order to take power) might be shaken by 'a fluidity, some flood'. In her book *Of Woman Born*, Adrienne Rich defines the modern patriarchal family with its

> supernaturalizing of the penis, its division of labour by gender, its emotional, physical and material possessiveness, its ideal of mono-gamous marriage until death (and its severe penalties for adultery by the wife), the 'illegitimacy' of a child born outside wedlock, the economic dependency of women, the unpaid domestic services of the wife, the obedience of women and children to male authority, the imprinting and continuation of heterosexual roles. (1977)

In privileging the womb, Luce Irigaray may be neglecting other aspects of female sexuality and biology which can be just as powerful. Irigaray's celebration of the womb and labia privilege (patriarchal/ masculinist) notions of motherhood, heterosexuality and female sexuality over other forms of sexuality. There are aspects of female sexuality which have not been considered by the French feminists – female ejaculation, for instance. The fluids that Irigaray and Julia Kristeva have appropriated in their form of sexual discourse are the fluids of the 'mother-body' (womb and birth fluids, menstrual blood, breast milk). The fluids of ejaculation have been handed over to masculinist discourse and the male body.[4] Female ejaculation is rendered 'invisible' in the dominant (masculinist) discourse, and even lesbian, queer and radical feminisms ignore it. It's much easier, and better, for patriarchal discourse to suppress forms of female sexuality such as female ejaculation, clitoral sex, lesbian sex, and so on, and to keep the primary metaphor for womanhood firmly maternal. This is the way patriarchal economy prefers to render female sexuality – in terms of motherhood, or 'compulsory heterosexuality'. It supports the patriarchal/ masculinist status quo.

Some feminists have loathed Luce Irigaray's view of female sexuality, because she over-emphasizes eroticism, at the expense of other aspects, according to Monique Plaza in ""Phallomorphic power" and the psychology of "woman"":

> All that 'is' woman comes to [Irigaray] in the last instances from her anatomical sex, which touches itself all the time. Poor woman. (32)

All right then: how about approaching Luce Irigaray's labial philosophy at the level of *metaphor*. There we score. There are problems in taking Irigaray too literally, just as people persist in taking the *Bible* literally, believing that God really did issue Ten Commandments, much as a press office releases statements on a senator's activities. As metaphor or poetry, Irigaray's psychoanalysis/ philosophy of the continually embracing sex lips is intriguing. This is an extract from Irigaray's essay "When Lips Speak Together" (with my interpolations):

> You speak from everywhere at the same time [*women's 'all-over' eroticism*]. You touch me whole at the same time [*touch as instant karma*]. In all senses [*synæsthesia*]. Why only one song, one discourse, one text at a time? [*a Rimbaudian question, the question of poetry as pure experience*] To seduce, satisfy, fill one of my 'holes'? [cp *the patriarchal view of women as 'three holes'*]. I don't have any, with you [*we are different, special*]. We are not voids, lacks which wait for sustenance, fulfilment, or plenitude from an other [*à la Lacan*]. That our [*labial/ sexual*] lips make us women does not mean that consuming, consummating, or being filled is what matters to us [*we do not ply the heterosexual, penetrative sexual mode*]. ("Lips", in M. Humm, 1992, 207)

Luce Irigaray, like Julia Kristeva and Hélène Cixous, has many modes of writing. When she is in her poetic mode, she can be mesmerizing. In her poetic voice, she is very positive and hopeful. The extract from "When Lips Speak Together" quoted above continues thus:

> Kiss me. Two lips kiss two lips [*labia against labia – a time-honoured cliché of lesbian sex in male pornography*], openness is ours again. Our 'world.' [*two lovers make a whole world*]. Between us [*just us, as lovers*], the movement from inside to outside, from outside to inside [*the transformation process*], knows no limits. It is without end [*the infinite*

self]. There are exchanges that no mark, no mouth can ever stop [*our sensuality will be limitless*]. Between us, the house has no walls, the clearing no enclosure, language no circularity [*space as metaphor loses its boundaries*]. You kiss me, and the world enlarges until the horizon vanishes [*love as infinity*]. (ib.)

This is expansive writing, writing which approaches the condition of the visionary. This is where Hélène Cixous and Luce Irigaray, and to a lesser extent Julia Kristeva, become inspiring. Kristeva's inspiring writing does not come so often from such deeply poetic modes. Even so, Kristeva does move into this lyrical mode in the bold face section of "Hérethique de l'amour" ("Stabat Mater").

The more one considers just what Luce Irigaray is saying in "When Our Lips Speak Together", the more one realizes just how utopian and visionary she is being here. She is saying: that we ('women') are not mere voids to be 'filled' by them ('men'); that between lovers a secret world is created which is also wholly outside as well as wholly inside; the further inside one goes, the further outside one goes; the exchange of lovers will be infinite; because when you kiss me the 'world enlarges until the horizon vanishes'; well, that is pure religious poetry. In Irigaray's system of two-lipped-togetherness, touch becomes infinite – the lips enable an expansion of movement that is unlimited. As she says: 'our pleasure consists of moving and being moved by each other, endlessly.' (ib.)

The emphasis on touch in Luce Irigaray's philosophy is part of her poetics of women's writing, which's a style that does not privilege sight, that emphasizes the tactile, that is simultaneous and 'always *fluid*' (*This Sex Which Is Not One*, I, 126). In this tactile simultaneity feminine 'style' is always fluid and beyond idealization and categorization. The dynamic derives from 'this friction between two infinitely neighbouring forces', so that woman's style 'resists and explodes all firmly established forms, figures, ideas, concepts' (ib., 76).

Chantal Chawaf, a contemporary French writer of Luce Irigaray's, also wrote of the physical fluidity of women's writing: 'I feel the political fecundity of mucus, milk, sperm, secretions which gush out to liberate energies and give them back to the world' (in M, 178). Irigaray reveres the womb-experience. She writes of the special relationship women have with their sexuality and morphology. In "Sexual Difference" (lecture, 1982), Irigaray remarks:

> Freud's statement that her stage is oral is significant but still exiles her from her most archaic and constituent site. No doubt the word 'oral' is particularly useful in describing a woman: morphologically she has two mouths and two pairs of lips. But she can only act on this morphology and create something from it if she retains her relationship to the *spatial* and the *foetal*. (I, 170)

The point to keep in mind when assessing Luce Irigaray's seemingly essentialist and biologist form of genital feminism is how much she insists on modes of relationship and representation, on how genital feminism relates to language and representation. For Irigaray, sexual difference 'conditions language and is conditioned by it' (Je, 20). Instead of phallocentric ways of representing and conceptualizing the world, Irigaray argues for new methods that oppose reductionism with openness, hierarchy with multiplicity, transcendence with immanence. Irigaray's quest for a metaphysics of sexual difference offers a new set of cultural models which would replace the hierarchical models of patriarchy, in which superiority and competition are dominant discourses. And for D.H Lawrence, the relation between the sexes is the main ethical problem of the modern era.

✤

In the 1980s, Luce Irigaray became increasingly concerned, like many feminists (including Hélène Cixous and Julia Kristeva), with the ethical, social and practical applications of feminist theory. Feminist critics, especially those in the Anglo-American camp, prefer feminist theory that can be turned into praxis. Easy to see how Irigaray's (and French feminism's) talk of a theoretical 'woman', instead of 'real women', would upset those feminists eager to overthrow patriarchy. In linguistic studies, such as *Parler n'est jamais neutre, Sexes et parentés, Sexes et genres à travers les langues* and *Le Langue des déments,* Irigaray explored the connections between speaking, language, art, æsthetics, gender, subject-ivity, identity and society. The vexed question of the relations between gender and social power was investigated in terms of linguistics: how much does the sex or gender of the speaking subject affect her/his social skills and influence? This is a controversial topic in feminism – Dale Spender, for example, in her feminist studies of gendered language (*Man Made Language,* 1980), women's history (*Women of Ideas,* 1982), and women's education (*Invisible Women,* 1982), and Shirley Ardener (*Women and Space,* 1981), Sheila Rowbotham (*Woman's Consciousness, Man's World,* 1973) and Deborah Cameron (*The Feminist Critique of Language,* 1990), have been severely criticized. Spender, for example, sometimes draws simplistic conclusions from her research. Feminists have not agreed on the ways in which gender relates to language (Spender, Rowbotham, Ardener, Susan McConnell-Giner, W.E.B. Du Bois, Toril Moi, Adrienne Rich, Nancy Henley, Hélène Cixous, Julia Kristeva, Robin Lakoff and Mary Daly, all differ in their approach to the relations between sex, gender and language).

So when it comes to social practice, there is little agreement among feminists other than in a general way. The evangelical nature of 'political correctness' (especially its tendency in the U.S.A. to veer into the ridiculous) has not helped either. Feminism has been roped into the 'political correctness' debate, which is largely unproductive. 'PC' is lambasted alike by the left and the right. Arguing about the validity of 'chair' instead of 'chairman' or a 'one person show' instead of a 'one man show' is all very well. But this is a tiny part of the debate surrounding language and gender. The man/ person sort of argument is an easy section of 'political correctness' to ridicule. As for a serious consideration in the media and press of the philosophical and theoretical aspects of language and gender, and its social implications, forget it.

For Luce Irigaray,

Man needs an instrument to touch himself: a hand, a woman, or some substitute. The replacement of that apparatus is effected in and through language. Man produces language for self-affection. And various forms of discourse, can be analysed as various modes of the auto-affect(at)ion of the 'subject'. (I, 58)

For Luce Irigaray the gender of the speaking subject became crucial: it was unethical to deny the gendered position. The entry into language (*pace* Freudian psychoanalysis) was gendered, and could not be abandoned. Indeed, Irigaray advocated an encouragement of sexual difference: this was one of the ways to change a social order. In this view, the links between speaking/ gender/ subjectivity and ethics/ society are very important: revealing the way men and women speak as gendered subjects uncovers the larger social system. Male narcissism is thus not confined to the Lacanian privileging of the phallus and the self-absorption of male sexuality, but to the wider issues of patriarchal power, language and society. Irigaray's linguistic analysis demonstrated that women's relations to selfhood were largely repressed: the same repressions were at work in the fields of science, health, the media, business, politics, education and philosophy. Language, as one of the central modes of representation, has to be addressed, in Irigaray's view, for a restructuring of society to occur. In this view, feminists' concern (anti-feminist critics would say obsession) with language is crucial.

Luce Irigaray's feminism continually hacks away at the conflicting demands of theory and practice, conceptual feminism and practical, social feminism. The conflicts can never quite be resolved, because the 'real', social world is full of far more problems than one feminist can consider. The real world simply does not fit in neatly to any single philosophic view, let alone a project of feminist social ethics. Thus, even as Irigaray attempts to solve the problems of the world which arise from gender, identity, linguistic and feminist issues, she is continually foxed by reality. And other feminists have shot holes in her theorizing.

Not least among Luce Irigaray's theories, the problem of sexual difference continues to cause controversy. It is perhaps Irigaray's insistence on the otherness of the other sex that annoys feminist critics. In Irigaray's forceful ethics of sexual difference, inter-relations between the sexes becomes founded on alterity, mutual respect and reciprocity. Irigaray uses the elements (earth, air, fire, water) and their continuous alchemical transformations as a model for the interactions that might take place between couples. In this model of interchange and merging, the two components may be able to produce something new which does not mean each loses their identity.

Perhaps the most unusual of Luce Irigaray's notions is of the divine, the sacred and religion. While major philosophers (such as Jacques Derrida and Roland Barthes), tend to sidestep religious issues (or at least, they come across as sceptical thinkers, who work independently of religions), Irigaray has spoken passionately of religion and the divine. For Irigaray, the religious sensibility is important. There has never been a 'constitution of subjectivity, or of any human society,' Irigaray writes in "Divine Women", 'which has been worked through without the help of the divine' (4). Instead of the Judæo-Christian God, the stern patriarchal Father figure of the West, Irigaray's gods are expressions or representations of feminine and masculine plenitude. The productivity of the masculine and feminine manifestations would not pivot around children and reproduction, but around creativity and love. Irigaray's sacred is thus a celebration of life, not a denial of life, and the relationships between the sexes.

✤

Luce Irigaray writes that '[m]en always go further, exploit further, seize more, without really knowing where they are going' (TD, 5). It can't be simply a case of 'blaming' men for everything, as Simone de Beauvoir said – blame men, yes, but blame 'the system' (society) also. Irigaray thinks that the abstraction 'equality' can only mean *at best* the equality of salaries, so that women will be paid the same as men; nothing else, Irigaray says, can be 'equal'; instead, there must eternal *difference*, in gender, from the sexual to the cultural. Irigaray says that difference must be emphasized, but her theory of difference is based, like the philosophy of Andrea Dworkin, on sexuality. Sexuality lies at the heart of the feminist discourse of feminists such as Dworkin, Irigaray, Hélène Cixous, Kate Millett, Susan Griffin and Shere Hite; they emphasize sexuality more than other factors, and this is a problem, this reduction, ultimately, to sexual matters. Donna C. Stanton has criticized Cixous' theories, seeing in them a return to the metaphysics of presence and identity, in which the technique of poetic metaphor suggests an economy of similitude, instead of one of difference (1986).

At times, Luce Irigaray seems to be like a French counterpart of Andrea Dworkin: Irigaray writes, so simply yet so effectively: 'there are no grounds for paying less for one body's work than for another's' (Je, 120). It's a view shared by Dworkin, who writes in *Letters From a War Zone*:

> Women who work earn fifty-six to fifty-nine cents on the dollar to what men get for comparable work... women get 100 per cent of the pregnancies, but only half the dollar.[5]

But Luce Irigaray does not believe in full 'equality', the only sort of equality she deems possible is economic, otherwise she argues for differ-ence, while acknowledging that '[w]hatever may be the inequalities between women, they all suffer, even unconsciously, the same oppression, the same exploitation of their body, the same denial of their desire'.[6]

All feminists agree that there is inequality and injustice in so many areas of life, but it's pointless always attacking men, because that is not the whole problem. It's pointless always attacking sexuality, for sexuality is only one part of human experience. Luce Irigaray is on to something when she argues for a 'culture of difference', because if you always resort to patriarchy and men you are always defining yourself and your concerns in terms of patriarchy and men. Thus women's sexuality is always compared to, contrasted with – and defined in terms of – male sexuality, which is clearly limiting, because you'll always be using masculinist or patriarchal terms.

Luce Irigaray's views on 'gender equality' (in *Je, tu, nous: Toward a Culture of Difference*) revolve around notions of women's sexual differ-ence:

> The demand to be equal presupposes a point of comparison. To whom

or to what do women want to be equalized? To men? To a salary? To a public office? To what standard? Why not to themselves? (Je, 12)

For Luce Irigaray, the exploitation of women derives from sexual difference, so the solution, she says, 'will only come through sexual difference' (Je, 12). Women's oppression and exploitation, says Irigaray, is incredible, bearing in mind where men come from.

> We still live in a framework of familio-religious relations in which the woman is the body to the man's head. It's quite astonishing that men, who in their cradle were totally dependent upon women and who owe their existence to this dependence, should then take the liberty of turning things around: men exist thanks to women's intelligence, but apparently women aren't capable of governing society or even of being full citizens... In an incredibly distrustful manœuvre, it's suspected that they would no longer want to protect life the moment they themselves have a right to it. Women are often nothing more than hostages of the reproduction of the species. (Je, 78)

Luce Irigaray published a number of more overtly politicized books in the 1980s and 1990s which dealt with the ethics of sexual difference: *Je, tu, nous: Toward a Culture of Difference, Thinking the Difference: For a Peaceful Revolution, Elemental Passions, Speech Is Never Neuter* and *An Ethics of Sexual Difference.*

In *Je, tu, nous: Toward a Culture of Difference,* Luce Irigaray argued passionately for a 'culture of difference' in gender. Instead of notions of 'equality', between men and women, so important to second wave/ 1970s feminism, Irigaray reckoned women need to be regarded as *different* – culturally, ideologically, psychologically, spiritually and sexually. Apart from equality in economics, men and women are different, or rather, women are different from men. In *Thinking the Difference: Towards a Peaceful Revolution,* Irigaray continued to develop her notions of 'difference'. The first essay was a speech given in 1986 in Tirrenia at the PCI (Partito communista italiano/ Italian Communist Party) conference. The anger in Irigaray's speech was sparked off by the nuclear accident at Chernobyl. One can agree with much of what Irigaray said about the culture of difference, and about the rigours of the patriarchal world. For example, Irigaray pointed out, coolly, that '[h]uge amounts of capital are allocated to the development of death machines in order to ensure peace' (4). She was right: it was a statement of fact, a fact which needed saying, and which had a new political resonance because of its context in a feminist philosophical speech. Irigaray went on to dismantle the nuclear argument with the coolness of a Bertrand Russell, but always speaking from a (female) feminist position.

For Luce Irigaray, the patriarchal nature of (our) culture was/is the creation of men. Whether Irigaray thought of men and women in cultural or actual terms, she came down, finally, on the essentialist/ biologist side. That is, she talked in terms of patriarchal *culture*, but also in terms of men and women. Though men and women may be patriarchally orientated, it is men, Irigaray claimed, not women, who have made the patriarchal culture. Like separatist feminists, Irigaray believed, though she did not say so directly, that if men did not exist society would not be patriarchal.

When in *Thinking the Difference* Luce Irigaray talked about the hideousness of noise pollution in our modern world, one agreed wholeheartedly: '[o]ur ears, constantly assaulted by the noise of machinery, including aircraft, no longer get any rest, and eventually become weaker in self-defence.' (22)

Luce Irigaray's post-Marxist analysis of society (bearing in mind she was speaking at an Italian Communist Party conference) – '[l]ife itself is treated like a commodity' (16) – was more suspect. It was too simplistic, too easy. Irigaray's account of earlier matriarchal societies, too, was nostalgic and incorrect. As with mythographers, poets and pagan writers such as Robert Graves, Robert Briffault, Monica Sjöo, Elinor Gadon, Caitlin Matthews, Marion Woodman and others, Irigaray forgot her acute critical faculties when she wrote of primitive/ ancient matriarchal cultures. For Irigaray, the mother is silenced and repressed in patriarchal culture: the mother is represented as the dark continent, and the relationship with the mother is the night, the shadow, hell. 'But men can no more, or rather no less, do without it than can women', Irigaray said in *Le*

Corps-à-corps avec la mère (1981). However, Irigaray's method of countering the representational hell of the mother – her suggestion that, to counter
contemporary social injustices, posters of mother-daughter couples should
be put up – is ridiculous (9). Irigaray was right to say that images of
mothers and daughters are few in the Western media landscape,[7] but
countering the rule of the Father with pictures of mothers and daughters is
hardly going to be enough. It is at times like these that Irigaray is quaint
and naïve. The idea of putting up posters of mothers and daughters (or
images of the Virgin Mary and her mother Anne for Christians) is cute to
entertain but is hardly going to revolutionize patriarchy. (Irigaray also
advocated lessons on love in schools: 'when will we teach [adolescents]
about love, exactly?' Irigaray fumed, suggesting that language lessons in
schools should include how to write a love letter, photographic exhib-
itions 'of girls or boys who are close friends, who are lovable or loved',
and art classes on imagining 'an outline or face of a dream lover' [Je,
104]). Oh, why isn't Irigaray President of the World – for laughs alone it
would be wonderful!

Luce Irigaray's thoughts, in *Thinking the Difference*, on matters such as
female identity, for instance, or the sensuality of touches, were enriching.
Anybody who could write, '[t]ouch, which plays a role in all the senses, is
a very special sense' (21), was worth listening to. Her writing in *Thinking
the Difference* on (female) subjectivity, on feeling, on the growth of female
sexuality, on pregnancy and the stages in a woman's life, was worthy and
full of insight. While so much of cultural studies wafts ever upward into
the clouds of abstraction and claustrophobic self-referentiality, Irigaray,
in the social ethics books, was refreshingly grounded in the body and the
senses. Her views were erratic, and even ludicrous at times, but her books
were challenging and enlightening. In *Thinking the Difference* she wrote:
'[n]ever abandon subjective experience as an element of knowledge' (30), a
sentence which scientists (and politicians) the world over might do well
to consider.

LUCE IRIGARAY

❧

Luce Irigaray argued passionately for a new openness, which she conceived, as so often, in morphologically metaphorical tones: 'woman', she said in "Divine Women", must break free of the metaphor of the watery envelope of the womb, and move out into the air.

> After the envelope full of water which was our pre-natal home, we have to construct, bit by bit, the envelope of air of our terrestrial space, air which is still free to breathe and sing, air where we deploy our appearances and our movements. We have been fishes. We will have to become birds. Which cannot be done without opening up and mobility in the air. (1986, 4)

In Luce Irigaray's work (as with Hélène Cixous' too), one often gets the feeling that she is straining at the bonds of some repression/ suppression/ oppression or other. Irigaray's works have a powerful sense of a desire for transcendence. Not simply for a 'progression' towards secular, political goals, such as equal rights or equal pay, but a spiritual, sensual transcendence, a moving up and out, symbolized here by the metaphor of transforming oneself from fish to bird, from water to air. Water is of the (maternal) past, pre-natal, nurturing, but always dependent on the mother; the air speaks of freedom of movement – in three dimensions, a much greater traversal of space than the fish seems to enjoy in water.

Luce Irigaray's use of metaphor pivots on notions of gendered symbolism: water ('feminine') and air ('masculine'). In Irigaray's form of *jouissance* or *extase*, a transcendent movement would traverse the boundaries between sacred and profane, being and non-being, inner and outer. In the new openness offered by concepts of 'difference', there may be no true 'inside' any longer: Jacques Derrida, discussing his conception of *différance*, wrote in *'Speech and Phenomena' and Other Essays on Husserl's Theory of Signs*:

> As soon as we admit spacing both as 'interval' or as difference and as openness upon the outside, there can no longer be any absolute inside. (86)

LUCE IRIGARAY

Luce Irigaray offers an openness which goes beyond Martin Heidegger's sense of 'the clearing'. Indeed, there is no end, no boundary to Irigaray's 'open'. Incorporating in her philosophy postmodern notions of emptiness and absence, Irigaray, like Julia Kristeva with her notions of the abject and marginal, is not at all negative or pessimistic. Joy rather than cynicism is the mark of her philosophy, which emphasizes the delight of the *risk* (the risk without which there can be nothing worthwhile, as Søren Kirkegaard said). Irigaray, in "La croyance même", conceives of two angels meeting face to face so they can share their new erotic space. The dare to love, to pursue transcendence, is crucial to Irigaray's philosophy, and is conceived in joyous terms: in *Le Oubli de l'air* she wrote:

> They who dare all go forth blindly, without projects. No longer spellbound by the fear of being without shelter. Unreservedly abandoning themselves to the unbounded open, holding nothing back. A flowering environment in which those who are free of all fear would be embraced. (I, 216)

In *Parler n'est jamais neutre*, Luce Irigaray wrote that

> the dance of the veil is the sexual and religious rite *par excellence*, a dance with a mystery and a cosmic reality that is at once prior to and beyond any already-constituted subjectivity. The scene is played out by the Mother-Gooddess or the Betrothed, the gods and the universe. It does not cover nothingness; it attempts to pass through the veil of illusion to reach the act/ gesture creating or begetting the world. (I, 87)

Part of Luce Irigaray's project, Alice Jardine says, is to dissect 'male texts' and invite women to 'join with her in desacralizing male theory and liberating while valorizing the feminine repressed in male texts' (1985, 262). Claire Duchen comments upon Irigaray's attack on masculinist culture: '[t]he phallogocentric desire for unity and linearity, for stable meaning, must be undermined on all fronts in many ways' (88).

For some critics and feminists (Elaine Showalter, Rachel Bowlby, Arleen Dallery, Mary Jacobus, Toril Moi, Janet Sayers, Ann Jones and Ellen Peel), Luce Irigaray's thought is too rigid and dogmatic, too biologist and essentialist, too dependent on a simplistic, ahistorical and fixed 'essence' of 'woman'.[8] Irigaray's thinking, however, cannot be compressed into a unified theory: she is playful, loves ventriloquizing other voices (such as Friedrich Nietzsche or Sigmund Freud), she likes to parody and rewrite other forms of discourse, and, like Hélène Cixous, loves puns.

The more sympathetic Irigarayan (feminist) critics have been those that have followed Luce Irigaray's thought as it develops over her works, without imposing unified or restrictive readings (Margaret Whitford, Naomi Schor, Elizabeth Grosz, Jane Gallop, Diana Fuss, Josette Féral and Carolyn Burke).[9] These critics see Irigaray's feminist strategic position as social, morphological, not essentialist and limiting. One thing's for sure about Luce Irigaray, though, she has provided feminists, philosophers and critics with plenty of material for continuing debate.

✤

ILLUSTRATIONS

❖

Images of some of the people who have influenced Lue Irigaray,
and people that she has studied.

On this page and the following pages
are some artists and thinkers discussed
by Luce Irigaray, and associated with her work.

Friedrich Nietzsche (below).

Sigmund Freud

Jacques Derrida, above.
Jacques Lacan, below.

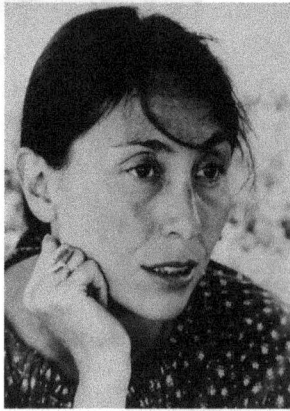

Julia Kristeva

Hélène Cixous

Monique Wittig

NOTES

PREFACE

1. S. Jackson: "Gender and Heterosexuality: A Materialist Feminist Analysis", in M. Maynard, 1994, 13.
2. S. Jackson, ib.; Christine Delphy: *The Main Enemy: A Materialist Analysis of Women's Oppression*, Women's Research and Resources Centre, 1977.
3. See Gayatri Chakravorty Spivak, 1981.
4. A. Huyssen, 1984, 16.

1. INTRODUCTORY

1. Katherine Stephenson, in E. Sartori, 230.

2. FRENCH FEMINIST POETICS

1. "A partir de *Polylogue*", interview with Françoise van Rossum-Guyon, *Revue des sciences humaines*, vol. XLIV, no. 168, tr. Seán Hand, Oct-Dec 1977, 495f.
2. Hélène Cixous: "Castration or Decapitation?", *Signs*, 7, 1, 52.
3. See Arleen B. Dallery; Deborah Cameron; Jan Montefiore; Andrea Nye:

"The voice of the serpent: French feminism and the philosophy of language", in A. Garry, 1989.

4. M. Wittig: "The Straight Mind", *Feminist Issues*, 1, 1, 110.

5. Luce Irigaray: *Parler n'est jamais neutre*, tr. David Macey, in I, 94.

6. Terry Eagleton: *Marxism and Literary Criticism*, University of California Press, Berkeley, CA, 1976, 34.

7. Marxist-Feminist Literature Collective: "Women's Writing: *Jane Eyre, Shirley, Villette, Aurora Leigh*", in Francis Barker *et al*, eds. *1848: The Sociology of Literature*, in M. Eagleton, 1986, 197.

8. Mary Ann Doane is sceptical: this seemingly desirable place of the French feminists is in fact a 'nonplace' (1988).

9. See, for example, Kelly Oliver: "Who is Nietzsche's Woman?", in B. On, 1994, and "Nietzsche's 'Woman'", *Radical Philosophy*, 48, 1988; Jean Graybeal: *Language and "the Feminine" in Nietzsche and Heidegger*, Indiana University Press, Bloomington 1990; D. Krell, 1986; D. O'Hara, 1985; Sarah Kofman: *Nietzsche et la scéne philosophique*, Union générale d'éditions, Paris, 1979; S. Kofman: "Baubô", in M. Gillespie; Carol Diethe: "Nietzsche and the Woman Question", *History of European Ideas*, 11, 1989; Gary Schapiro: *Alcyone: Nietzsche on Gifts, Noise, and Women*, State University of New York Press , Albany 1991; O. Schutte: "Nietzsche on Gender Difference", in B. On; Michael Platt: "Woman, Nietzsche, and Nature", *Maieutis*, 2, 1981; Gayle L. Ormiston: "Traces of Derrida: Nietzsche's Image of Woman", *Philosophy Today*, 28, 1984; L. Baker, 1989; E. Behler, 1988.

10. J. Derrida, *Spurs*, 101; see also D. Krell, 1986.

11. See Kelly Oliver; Sarah Kofman, op. cit.

12. F. Nietzsche: *Briefe an Peter Gast*, Leipzig, 1924, 89-90.

13. Janet Lungstrum: "Nietzsche Writing Woman/ Woman Writing Nietzsche", in P. Burgard, 144.

14. Sarah Kofman: *L'Enigma de la femme: La femme dans les textes de Freud*, Galilée, Paris, 1980. See also Biddy Martin: *Woman and Modernity: The (Life)Styles of Lou Andreas-Salomé*, Cornell University Press, Ithaca 1991.

15. L. Andreas-Salomé: "Die in sich ruhende Frau", in *Zur Psychologie der Frau*, ed. Giselda Brinker-Gabler, Fischer, Frankfurt, 1978, 295-6.

16. Both Arkady Plotinsky and Alan D. Schrift use Hélène Cixous' ecstatic text "The Laugh of the Medusa", and "Sorties" (A. Plotinsky: "The Medusa's Ears: The Question of Nietzsche, the Question of Gender, and Transformation of Theory"; A. Schrift: "On the Gynecology of Morals: Nietzsche and Cixous on the Logic of the Gift", both in P. Burgard, 1994).

17. See John Lechte: "Art, Love, and Melancholy in the Work of Julia

Kristeva", in J. Fletcher, 39.

18. Kelly Oliver: "Nietzsche's Abjection", in P. Burgard, 60.
19. F. Nietzsche: *The Birth of Tragedy*, tr. W. Kaufmann, Vintage, New York, 1967, §16, p. 104.
20. Benjamin Bennett: "Bridge: Against Nothing", in P. Burgard, 308.
21. F. Nietzsche: *Ecce Homo*, in *On the Genealogy of Morals and Ecce Homo*, Vintage, New York, N.Y., 1967, 266.
22. See P. Burgard, 235; see also S. Kofman, D. A. Schrift, J. Lungstrum, *et al*, in the same volume; also, Hélène Cixous' "Sorties" and *Newly-Born Woman*.
23. F. Nietzsche: *The Gay Science*, tr. Walter Kaufmann, Vintage, New York, 1974, §72, p. 129.
24. Luce Irigaray: *Speculum of the Other Woman*, tr. Gillian C. Gill, and *This Sex Which Is Not One*, tr. Catherine Porter, both Cornell University Press, New York, N.Y., 1985; see also: Dorothy Leland: "Lacanian psychoanalysis and French feminism: toward an adequate political psychology", *Hypatia*, 3, 3, Winter 1989, 81-103.
25. Elizabeth Grosz: "Refiguring Lesbian Desire", in L. Doan, 75.
26. R.M. Rilke, letter to Clara Rilke, 8 March 1907, in *Gesammalte Briefe 1892-1926*, Insel Verlag, Leipzig 1940, II, 279f.
27. Maggie Humm: "Is the gaze feminist? Pornography, film and feminism", *Perspectives on Pornography*, eds. G. Day & C. Bloom, Macmillan 1988; L. Gamman, 1988; E.D. Pribram, 1988.
28. J. Lacan, "The meaning of the phallus", 1988; Bernard Baas: "Le désir pur", *Ornicar?*, 83, 1987; R. Lapsley, 1992.
29. C. Jung: *The Development of Personality*, vol. 17, Routledge, London, 1954, 198; Marie-Louise von Franz: *The Psychological Meaning of Redemption Motifs in Fairy Tales*, Inner City Books, Toronto 1980, 39f.
30. Emma Jung & Marie-Louise von Franz: *The Grail Legend*, tr. Andrea Dykes, Sigo Press, Boston, Mass., 1980, 64.
31. Hélène Cixous writes: '[m]en say that there are two unrepresentable things: death and the feminine sex. That's because they need femininity to be associated with death; it's the jitters that give them a hard-on! For themselves! They need to be afraid of us.' ("The Laugh of the Medusa", M, 255) .
32. Larysa Mykyta: "Lacan, Literature and the Look", *SubStance*, 39, 1983, 54.
33. See Laura Mulvey: "Visual pleasure and narrative cinema", *Screen*, vol. 16, no. 3, 1975, 6-19.
34. Catherine King: "The Politics of Representation: A Democracy of the Gaze", in F. Bonner *et al*, eds. *Imagining Women Cultural Representations and Gender*, Polity Press, Cambridge, 1992, 136.

35. Luce Irigaray, "Women's Exile", in D. Cameron, 1990, 83; and Luce Irigaray: *Speculum*.
36. T. Moi, 1985, 134.
37. Emma Pérez: "Irigaray's Female Symbolic in the Making of Chicana Lesbian *Sitios y Lenguas (Sites and Discourses)*", in L. Doan, 108.
38. C. Weedon, 1987, 63; D. Stanton, 1986, 160; M. Plaza, 1978; J. Sayers, 1986, 42; B. Brown, 1979, 38.

3. LUCE IRIGARAY, FRENCH FEMINISM, SEXUALITY, AND SEXUAL DIFFERENCE

1. Xavière Gauthier, in M, 201-2.
2. L. Irigaray: "Ce sexe qui n'en est pas un", M, 103; see also: Jane Gallop, 1983, 77-83; Elizabeth Grosz: "Philosophy, subjectivity and the body", in C. Pateman & E. Grosz, 1986, 125-43.
3. Moira Gatens: "Power, Bodies and Difference", in M. Barrett, 1992, 134.
4. A. Jones: "Writing the Body", in E. Showalter, ed., 369.
5. Audre Lorde: *Sister Outsider*, Crossing Press, New York, N.Y., 1984, and in M. Humm 1992, 283.
6. Sue Miller: *The Good Mother*, Harper & Row, New York, N.Y., 1986.
7. Summer Brenner: *The Soft Room*, Figures 1978.
8. Susan Griffin: *Viyella*, in Laura Chester, 326.
9. See, for instance, Lonnie Barbach, ed. *Pleasures: Women Write Erotica*, Doubleday, New York, N.Y., 1984; Laura Duesing: *Three West Coast Women*, Five Fingers Poetry, 1987; Clayton Eshleman, ed. *Caterpillar Anthology*, Anchor 1971; Lynne Tillman: *Weird Fucks*, 1980; Jane Hirshfield: *Of Gravity and Angels*, Wesleyan University Press 1988; Jayne Anne Phillips: *Black Tickets*, Delacorte Press 1979; Marilyn Hacker: *Love, Death and the Changing of the Seasons*, Arbor House 1986; Nancy Friday: *Forbidden Flowers: More Women's Sexual Fantasies*, Arrow 1993.
10. Xavière Gauthier, in M, 201-2.
11. Catherine MacKinnon: "Feminism, Marxism, Method, and the State: An Agenda for Theory", in N.O. Keohane, ed. *Feminist Theory: A Critique of Ideology*, Harvester, 1982.
12. Elaine Marks, "Lesbian Intertextuality", in G. Stambolian, 376.
13. Marilyn Farewell: "Toward Definition of the Lesbian Literary Imagination", *Signs*, 14, 1988, 98.
14. Namascar Shaktini: "Displacing the Phallic Subject: Wittig's Lesbian Writing", *Signs*, 8, 1, Autumn 1982, 29.

15. Dianne Chisholm: "Lesbianism", in E. Wright, 1992, 217.
16. See Marina Warner, *Monuments and Maidens,* Weidenfeld & Nicholson, London, 1985; Kenneth Clark: *The Nude,* Pantheon Books, 1957; Lynda Nead, 19 .
17. Sherry B. Ortner, 1982.
18. See J. Still, 1993, 14f; D. Stanton; Annie Leclerc: *Parole de femme,* Paris 1974.
19. Myra Jehlen: "Archimedes and the paradox of feminist criticism", *Signs,* 6, 4, 1981, 575f.
20. Edwin Ardener: "Belief and the Problem of Women", in Shirley Ardener, ed. *Perceiving Women,* Halsted Press, New York, N.Y., 1978.
21. Elaine Showalter: "Feminist Criticism in the Wilderness", in E. Showalter, 1986, 262-3; J. Roberts, 1991, 1-5.
22. Sherry B. Ortner, 1982.
23. Ann Rosalind Jones: "Writing the Body: L'Écriture féminine", in E. Showalter, 1986, 363.
24. A. Jardine, "Opaque Texts", in N. Miller, 1986, 109.
25. Victor Burgin: "Geometry and Abjection", in J. Fletcher, 115-6.
26. Luce Irigaray: "La différence sexuelle", *Ethiope de la différence sexuelle,* Minuit, Paris, 1984, and in Toril Moi, 1988, 128.
27. J. Kristeva: "La femme, ce n'est jamais ça", *Tel Quel,* Autumn 1974, in M, 135.
28. S. Hekman, 1990, 42.
29. C. Burke, 1981, 289; J. Sayers, 1982, 132; C. Faure, 1981, 85.
30. M. Duras, interview in *Signs,* Winter 1975, in M, 175.
31. For Griselda Pollock, Julia Kristeva's emphasis in her æsthetics of painting on the 'feminine' encourages seeing 'woman as difference, inchoate, unspeakable, enigmatic, metaphor for all that is outside representation and meaning except as lack' ("Painting, Feminism, History", in M. Barrett, 1992, 157).
32. See Gayatri Spivak, in M. Krupnick, 177.
33. See Susan Rubin Suleiman: "(Re)Writing the Body: The Politics of Female Eroticism", in S. Suleiman, 14f; Elizabeth Grosz, 1988, 28-33; Alison M. Jaggar, 1989; Naomi Schor, 1989, 38-58.
34. Monique Witting: "One Is Not Born a Woman", speech at the Feminist as Scholar Conference, May 1979, Barnard College, New York.
33. E. Showalter: "Feminist Criticism in the Wilderness", in E. Showalter, ed., 250.
35. In V. Conley, 1984, 57.
36. French feminists, such as Hélène Cixous and Luce Irigaray, do not claim to 'represent' *all* women or 'women' as a concept (M. Gatens, in M. Barrett, 1992, 134).

37. R. DuPlessis, 1986, 273; S. Gilbert, 1986, xvi; M. Hite, 1988, 123.

4. LUCE IRIGARAY'S PHILOSOPHY OF SEXUAL DIFFERENCE

1. Naomi Schor; 1985; J. Still, 1993, 32.
2. Shoshana Felman: "The critical phallacy", *Diacritics*, Winter 1975, 3.
3. Collected in *Le Corps-à-corps avec la mère* (translated as "Women-mothers: the silent substratum of the social order"), I, 48.
4. Shannon Bell: "Feminist Ejaculations", in A. Kroker, 1991, 152-3; Chris Straayer: "The Seduction of Boundaries: Feminist Fluidity in Annie Sprinkle's Art/ Education/ Sex", in P. Gibson, 1993.
5. A. Dworkin, *Letters From a War Zone*, 145.
6. Luce Irigaray, "Women's Exile", in D. Cameron, 1990, 83.
7. See Claire Buck: ""O Careless, Unspeakable Mother": H.D, Irigaray, and Maternal Origin", in S. Sellers, 1991, 142.
8. Rachel Bowlby: "The Feminine Female", *Social Text*, 7, 1983; A. Dallery 1989; M. Jacobus 1986; T. Moi 1985; A. Jones 1981; E. Peel 1986; Janet Sayers: *Sexual Contradictions*, Tavistock 1986; E. Showalter 1986.
9. J. Gallop 1983; M. Whitford 1986, 1991; E. Grosz 1989; N. Schor 1989; C. Burke, 1981; J. Féral: "Antigone or the Irony of the Tribe", *Diacritics*, 8, 2, Autumn 1978 and "Towards a Theory of Displacement", *SubStance*, 1981; D. Fuss, 1989.

BIBLIOGRAPHY

Titles in English are published in London, England, unless otherwise stated. Titles in French are published in Paris, France, unless otherwise stated.

LUCE IRIGARAY

This Sex Which Is Not One, tr. C. Porter & C. Burke, Cornell University Press, New York, 1977

Speculum of the Other Woman, tr. G.C. Gill, Cornell University Press, New York, 1985

The Irigaray Reader, ed. Margaret Whitford, Blackwell, Oxford, 1991

Marine Lover of Friedrich Nietzsche, tr. G.C. Gill, Columbia University Press, New York, 1991

Elemental Passions, Athlone, London, 1992

Je, tu, nous: Toward a Culture of Difference, tr. Alison Martin, Routledge, London, 1993

An Ethics of Sexual Difference, Athlone, London, 1993

I Love to You: Sketch for a Felicity Within History, 1990, tr. 1993

Thinking the Difference: For a Peaceful Revolution, Athlone Press, London,

1994

Speech is Never Neuter, Athlone, London, 1994
"Ecce Mulier?", tr. Madeline Dobie, *Graduate Faculty Journal*, 15, 2, 1991, in P. Burgard, 1994
Democracy Begins Between Two, 1994, tr. 2000
To Be Two, 1997, tr. 2001
Between East and West, 1999, tr. 2001
The Way of Love, Paris, 2002
Sharing the World, tr. 2008
Conversations, Continuum, 2008
Luce Irigaray Teaching, Continuum, 2008
In the Beginning She Was, Continuum, 2012

Speculum de l'autre femme, Minuit, Paris, 1974
Ce Sexe qui n'en pas un, Minuit, Paris, 1977
Et l'une ne bouge pas sans l'autre, Minuit, Paris, 1979
Le Corps-à-corps avec la mère, La Pleine Lune, Ottawa, 1981
Passions élémentaires, Minuit, Paris, 1982
La Croyance même, Galilée, Paris, 1983
L'Oubli de l'air: Chez Martin Heidegger, Minuit, Paris, 1983
Ethique de la différence sexuelle, Minuit, Paris, 1984
Parler n'est jamais neutre, Minuit, Paris, 1985
Sexes et parentés, Minuit, Paris, 1987
Le Temps de la différence, Livre de Poche, Paris, 1989
J'aime à toi: Esquisse d'une félicité dans l'histoire, Grasset, Paris, 1992
Sexes et genres à travers les langues, Grasset, Paris, 1995

"When Our Lips Speak Together", *Signs*, 6, 1, Autumn, 1980
interview with Heather Jon Maroney: "Language, Persephone and Sacrifice", *Borderlines*, 4, 1985-6
"Divine Women", tr. Stephen Muecke, *Local Consumption: Occasional Papers*, 4, 1986
"Women, the Sacred and Money", tr. Diana Knight & Margaret Whitford, *Paragraph*, 8, 1986
"The Fecundity of the Caress", in R. Cohen, 1986
interview, in Janet Todd Baruch, 1988
"Equal to Whom?", *differences*, 1, 1989
interview, "Equal to whom?", *differences*, 1, 2, 1989
interview, in R. Mortley, 1991

OTHERS

Keith Ansell-Pearson & Howard Caygill, eds. *The Fate of the New Nietzsche*, Avebury, 1993

Alison Assister. *Althusser and Feminism*, Pluto Press, London, 1990

—. & Avedon Carol, eds. *Bad Girls and Dirty Pictures: The Challenge to Reclaim Feminism*, Pluto Press, London, 1993

Margaret Attack. "The Other Feminist", *Paragraph*, 8, 1986

—. & Phil Powrie, eds. *Contemporary French Fiction by Women*, Manchester University Press, 1990

Lang Baker. "Irigaray contre Bataille: Locating the Feminine in Nietzsche", *Social Discourse*, 2, 1989

Francis Barker *et al*, eds. *The Politics of Theory: The Proceedings of the Essex Conference on the Psychology of Literature*, University of Essex, Colchester, 1983

Michèle Barrett & Anne Phillips, eds. *Destablizing Theory: Contemporary Feminist Debates*, Polity Press, London, 1992

Roland Barthes. *Mythologies*, Hill & Wang, New York, 1972

—. *S/Z*, Hill and Wang, New York, 1974

—. *The Pleasure of the Text*, Hill and Wang, New York, 1975

—. *Image, Music, Text*, tr. Stephen Heath, Fontana, London, 1984

Elaine Hoffman Baruch & Lucienne Serrano: *Women Analyse Women in France, England and the United States*, Harvester Wheatsheaf, Hemel Hempstead, Herts., 1988

Ruth Behar, ed. *Women Writing Culture*, University of California Press, 1995

Ernst Behler. *Derrida – Nietzsche/ Nietzsche – Derrida*, Schöningh, Munich, 1988

Catherine Belsey. *Critical Practice*, Routledge, London, 1980

—. *Desire: Love Stories in Western Culture*, Blackwell, Oxford, 1994

Mary Berg. "Escaping the Cave: Luce Irigaray and Her Feminist Critics", in Gary Wihl & David Williams, eds. *Literature and Ethics*, McGill, Kingston, 1988

Philippa Berry & Andrew Wernick, eds. *Shadow of Spirit: Postmodernism and Religion*, Routledge, London, 1992

E. Brater, ed. *Feminine Focus: The New Women Playwrights*, Oxford University Press, 1989

Teresa Brennan, ed. *Between Feminism and Psychoanalysis*, Routledge, London, 1989

Peter Brooker, ed. *Modernism/ Postmodernism*, Longman, London, 1992

L. Brouwer *et al*, eds. *Beyond Limits*, University of Groningen Press,

Groningen, 1990

B. Brown & P. Adams. "The feminine body and feminist politics", *M/F*, 3, 1979

Wendy Brown. "Hesitations, Postmodern Exposures", *differences*, 3, 1, 1991

David Buckingham, ed. *Reading Audiences*, Manchester University Press, 1995

Peter J. Burgard, ed. *Nietzsche and the Feminine*, University Press of Virginia, Charlottesville, 1994

Victor Burgin *et al*, eds. *Formations of Fantasy*, Methuen, London, 1986

Carolyn C. Burke. "Rethinking the maternal", in H. Eisenstein, 1980

—. "Irigaray Through the Looking Glass", *Feminist Studies*, 2, Summer, 1981

Judith Butler. *Gender Trouble: Feminism and the Subversion of Identity*, Routledge, London, 1990

—. & J.W. Scott, eds. *Feminists Theorise the Political*, Routledge, London, 1992

Colette Camelin. "La Scène de la fille dans *Illa*", *Littérature*, 67, October, 1987

Deborah Cameron, ed. *The Feminist Critique of Language: A Reader*, Routledge, London, 1990

Claudia Card, ed. *Adventures in Lesbian Philosophy*, Indiana University Press, 1994

Gail Chester & Julienne Dickey, ed. *Feminism and Censorship: The Current Debate*, Prism Press, Bridport, Dorset, 1988

Laura Chester, ed. *Deep Down: New Sensual Writing By Women*, Faber, 1987

Hélène Cixous. *The Newly Born Woman*, tr. Betsy Wing, Minnesota University Press, Minneapolis, 1986

—. *"Coming to Writing" and Other Essays*, tr. Sarah Cornell *et al*, Harvard University Press, Cambridge, 1991

—. *Three Steps on the Ladder of Writing*, tr. Sarah Cornell & Susan Sellers, Columbia University Press, New York, 1993

—. *The Hélène Cixous Reader*, ed. Susan Sellers, Blackwell, Oxford, 1994

Richard A. Cohen, ed. *Face to Face with Levinas*, State University of New York Press, Albany, 1986

Alex Comfort. *I and That*, Beazley, 1979

Verena Andermatt Conley. "Julia Kristeva and the Traversal of Modern Poetic Space", *Enclitic*, 1, 1977

—. "Hélène Cixous and the Uncovery of Feminine Language", *Women and Literature*, 7, 1, 1977

—. *Hélène Cixous: Writing the Feminine*, University of Nebraska Press,

Lincoln 1984

—. ed. *Boundary* 2, 12, Winter, 1984, Cixous number

—. *Hélène Cixous: Writing the Feminine*, University of Nebraska Press, Lincoln 1991

—. *Hélène Cixous*, Harvester Wheatsheaf, Hemel Hempstead, Herts., 1992

Diane Griffin Crowder. "Amazons and mothers? Monique Wittig, Hélène Cixous and theories of women's writing", *Contemporary Literature*, 24, Summer, 1983

Arleen Dallery. "The Politics of Writing (the) Body: *Écriture Féminine*", in A. Jaggar, 1989

Mary Daly. *Pure Lust: Elemental Feminist Philosophy*, Women's Press, 1984

G. Day & C. Bloch, eds. *Perspectives on Pornography: Sexuality in Film and Literature*, Macmillan, London, 1988

Jacques Derrida. *'Speech and Phenomena' and Other Essays on Husserl's Theory of Signs*, tr. David B. Allison, Northwestern University Press, Evanston, 1973

—. *Of Grammatology*, John Hopkins University Press, Baltimore, 1976

—. *Spurs: Nietzsche's Styles*, University of Chicago Press, Chicago, IL, 1979

—. *Writing and Difference*, University of Chicago Press, 1987

Laura Doan, ed. *The Lesbian Postmodern*, Columbia University Press, New York, 1994

Mary Ann Doane. *The Desire to Desire: The Woman's Film of the 1940's*, Macmillan, London, 1988

Claire Duchen. *Feminism in France From May '68 to Mitterand*, Routledge, London, 1986

—. ed. *French Connections: Voices From the Women's Movement in France*, Hutchinson, London, 1987

Rachel DuPlessis. "For the Etruscans", in E. Showalter, 1986

J. Duran. *Toward a Feminist Epistemology*, Savage, Rowman & Littlefield, 1991

Andrea Dworkin. *Pornography: Men Possessing Women*, Women's Press, London, 1984

—. *Intercourse*, Arrow, London, 1988

Mary Eagleton, ed. *Feminist Literary Criticism*, Longman, London, 1991

—. ed. *Feminist Literary Theory: A Reader*, Blackwell, Oxford, 1986

Hester Eisenstein & Alice Jardine, eds. *The Future of Difference*, Barnard College Women's Center, New York, 1980

—. *Contemporary Feminist Thought*, Unwin Paperbacks, London, 1984

M. Ellman, ed. *Thinking about Women*, Virago, London, 1979

Christine Faure. "The twilight of the goddesses, or the intellectual crisis of

French feminism", *Signs*, 7, 1981

R. Felski. *Beyond Feminist Aesthetics: Feminist Literature and Social Change*, Hutchinson, London, 1989

Josette Féral. "Antigone or the irony of the tribe", *Diacritics*, Autumn, 1978

—. "The Powers of Difference", in H. Eisenstein, 1980

John Ferguson. *An Illustrated Encyclopædia of Mysticism*, Thames & Hudson, 1976

John Fletcher & Andrew Benjamin, eds. *Abjection, Melancholia and Love: the Work of Julia Kristeva*, Routledge, London, 1990

Penny Florence & Dee Reynolds, eds. *Feminist subjects, multi-media: Cultural methodologies*, Manchester University Press, 1995

Sigmund Freud. *Standard Edition of the Complete Psychological Works of Sigmund Freud*, 24 vols, ed. James Strachey, Hogarth Press, London, 1953-74

Diana Fuss. *Essentially Speaking*, Routledge, New York, 1989

—. ed. *Inside/ Out: Lesbian Theories, Gay Theories*, Routledge, London, 1991

Jane Gallop. *Feminism and Psychoanalysis: the daughter's seduction*, Macmillan, 1982

—. "*Quand nos lèvres s'écrivent*: Irigaray's body politic", *Romantic Review*, 74, 1983

—. *Thinking Through the Body*, Columbia University Press, New York, 1988

Lorraine Gamman & Margaret Marshment, eds. *The Female Gaze: Women as Viewers of Popular Culture*, Women's Press, London, 1988

Ann Garry & Marilyn Pearsal, eds. *Women, Knowledge and Reality: explorations in feminist philosophy*, Unwin Hyman, London, 1989

Xavière Gauthier. "Pourquoi Sorcières?", in *Sorcières*, 1, 1976, in E. Marks, 1981

Serge Gavronsky, ed. *Toward a New Poetics: Contemporary Writing in France*, University California Press, Berkeley, CA, 1994

Elissa D. Gelfand & Virginia Thorndike Hules: *French Feminist Criticism*, Garland, New York, 1985

Anna Gibbs. "Cixous and Gertrude Stein", *Meanjin*, 38, 1979

Pamela Church Gibson & Roma Gibson, ed. *Dirty Looks: Women, Pornography, Power*, British Film Institute, London, 1993

Sandra Gilbert. "A tarantella of history", introduction to Cixous, *The Newly Born Woman*

M.A. Gillespie & T.B. Strong, eds. *Nietzsche: Explorations in Philosophy, Aesthetics, and Politics*, University of Chicago Press, Chicago, IL, 1988

Gayle Greene & Coppélia Kahn, eds. *Making a Difference: Feminist Literary Criticism*, Methuen, London, 1985

Gabriele Griffin, ed. *Outwrite: Lesbianism and Popular Culture*, Pluto Press, London, 1993

—. *et al*, eds. *Stirring It: Challenges For Feminism*, Taylor & Francis, London, 1994

Morwenna Griffiths & Margaret Whitford, eds. *Feminist Perspectives in Philosophy*, Indiana University Press, Bloomington, IN, 1988

Elizabeth Grosz. "Irigaray and Sexual Difference", *Australian Feminist Studies*, 2, 1986

—. "Philosophy, Subjectivity and the Body", in C. Pateman, 1986

—. "Desire, the body and recent French feminism", *Intervention*, 21-2, 1988

—. *Sexual Subversions*, Allen & Unwin, London, 1989

—. "Lesbian fetishism?", *differences*, 3, 2, 1991

—. "Fetishization", in E. Wright, 1992

—. "Julia Kristeva", in E. Wright, 1992

—. *Volatile Bodies*, Indiana University Press, Bloomington, IN, 1994

—. "Refiguring Lesbian Desire", in L. Doan, 1994

—. *Space, Time and Perversion*, Routledge, London, 1995

Susan J. Hekman. *Gender and Knowledge: Elements of a Postmodern Feminism*, Polity Press, London, 1990

Molly Hite. "Writing – and reading – the body: female sexuality and recent feminist fiction", *Feminist Studies*, 14, 1, 1988

Christine Holmlund. "I Love Luce: The Lesbian, Mimesis and Masquerade in Irigaray, Freud, and Mainstream Film", *New Formations*, 8, Autumn, 1989

Maggie Humm. *Feminisms: A Reader*, Harvester Wheatsheaf, Hemel Hempstead, Herts., 1992

—. ed. *The Dictionary of Feminist Theory*, Harvester Wheatsheaf, Hemel Hempstead, Herts., 1995

Andreas Huyssen. "Mapping the postmodern", *New German Critique*, 33, 1984

—. *After the Great Divide: Modernism, Mass Culture, Postmodernism*, Indiana University Press, Bloomington, IN, 1986

Hypatia, 3, 3, 1989, French feminism issue

Mary Jacobus, ed. *Women Writing and Writing About Women*, Croom Helm, 1979

—. "Is There a Woman In This Text?", *New Literary History*, 14, 1982

—. *Reading Woman: essays in feminist criticism*, Methuen, London, 1986

—. "Madonna: Like a Virgin, or, Freud, Kristeva, and the Case of the Missing Mother", *Oxford Literary Review*, 8, 1986

A. Jaggar & S.R. Bordo, eds. *Gender/ Body/ Knowledge: Feminist Reconstructions of Being and Knowing*, Rutgers University Press, New Brunswick, 1989

Alice Jardine. *Gynesis,* Cornell University Press, New York, 1985

—. "Opaque Texts", in N. Miller, 1986

—. & Anne M. Menke. "Exploding the Issue: 'French' 'Women' 'Writers' and 'the Canon'?", *Yale French Studies*, 75, 1988

—. & Anne M. Menke, eds. *Shifting Scenes: interviews on women, writing and politics in post '68 France*, Columbia University Press, New York, 1991

Karla Jay, ed. *Lesbian Erotics*, New York University Press, 1995

Ann Rosalind Jones. "Julia Kristeva on femininity: the limits of a semiotic politics", *Feminist Review*, 18, Winter, 1984

—. "Writing the Body: Toward an Understanding of L'Écriture féminine", in E. Showalter, 1986

Jordan Jones. "Renewing the Dance: René Daumal, the Surrealism of the Bardo, and Shamanic Poetry", *Heaven Bone*, 11, Spring, 1994

C.G. Jung. *Memories, Dreams, Reflections*, Collins, London, 1967

Laura Kipnis. "Feminism: the Political Conscience of Postmodernism?", in P. Brooker, 1992

Vivian Kogan. "I Want Vulva! Hélène Cixous and the Poetics of the Body", *L'Esprit créateur*, 25, 2, Summer, 1985

David Farrell Krell. *Postponement: Women, Sensuality, and Death in Nietzsche-Interpretation*, Routledge, London, 1988

Julia Kristeva. *About Chinese Women*, tr. A. Barrows, Boyars, London, 1977

—. *Polylogue*, Seuil, Paris, 1977

—. *Powers of Horror: An Essay on Abjection*, tr. Leon S. Roudiez, Columbia University Press, New York, 1982

—. *Desire in Language: A Semiotic Approach to Literature and Art*, ed. Leon S. Roudiez, tr. Thomas Gora *et al*, Blackwell, Oxford, 1982

—. *Revolution in Poetic Language*, tr. Margaret Walker, Columbia University Press, New York, 1984

—. *The Kristeva Reader*, ed. Toril Moi, Blackwell, Oxford, 1986

—. *Tales of Love*, tr. Leon S. Roudiez, Columbia University Press, New York, 1987

—. *Black Sun: Depression and Melancholy*, tr. Leon S. Roudiez, Columbia University Press, New York, 1989

—. "A Question of Subjectivity: an interview" [with Susan Sellers], *Women's Review*, 12, 1986, in P. Rice, 1992

Eléanor Kuykendall. "Toward an Ethic of Nurturance: Luce Irigaray on Mothering and Power", in Joyce Trebilcot, ed. *Mothering: Essays in Feminist Theory*, Rowman & Allanheld, NJ, 1984

Jacques Lacan and the École Freudienne. *Écrits: A Selection*, tr. Alan

Sheridan, Tavistock, 1977

—. *Feminine Sexuality*, ed. Juliet Mitchell and Jacqueline Rose, Macmillan, London, 1988

D. Landry & G. MacLean. *Unbearable Weight*, Blackwell, Oxford, 1993

Rob Lapsley & Michael Westlake. "From *Casablanca* to *Pretty Woman*: the Politics of Romance", *Screen*, 33, 1, Spring 1992

Teresa de Laurentis, ed. *Feminist Studies/ Critical Studies*, Macmillan, 1988

John Lechte. *Julia Kristeva*, Routledge, London, 1990 (a)

—. "Art, Love, and Melancholy in the Work of Julia Kristeva", in J. Fletcher, 1990 (b)

S. Lefanu. *In the Chinks of the World Machine: Feminism and Science Fiction*, Women's Press, London, 1988

Philip Lewis. "Revolutionary Semiotics", *Diacritics*, 4, 3, Autumn, 1974

Cecile Lindsay. "Body Language: French Feminist Utopias", *The French Review*, 60, 1, October, 1986

JoAnn Loulan. *The Lesbian Erotic Dance: Butch, Femme, Androgyny, and Other*, Spinsters, San Francisco, 1990

Juliet Flower MacCannell, ed. *The Other Perspective in Gender and Culture: Rewriting Women and the Symbolic*, Columbia University Press, New York, 1990

Christiane Makward. "Interview with Hélène Cixous", *SubStance*, 5, 1976

Elaine Marks & Isabelle de Courtivron, eds. *New French Feminisms: an Anthology*, Harvester Wheatsheaf, Hemel Hempstead, Herts., 1981

M. Maynard & J. Purvis, eds. *Researching Woman's Lives*, Taylor & Francis, London, 1994

Geraldine Meaney. *(Un)Like Subjects: Women, Theory, Fiction*, Routledge, London, 1993

Elaine Millard. "French Feminisms", in S. Mills, 1989

N.K. Miller, ed. *The Poetics of Gender*, Columbia University Press, New York, 1986

Kate Millett. *Sexual Politics*, Doubleday, Garden City, 1970

Sara Mills *et al*, eds. *Feminist Readings/ Feminists Reading*, University Press of Virginia, Charlottesville, 1989

—. ed. *Gendering the Reader*, Harvester Wheatsheaf, Hemel Hempstead, Herts., 1993

Toril Moi. *Sexual/ Textual Politics: Feminist Literary Theory*, Routledge, London, 1988

—. ed. *French Feminist Thought*, Blackwell, Oxford, 1988

Jan Montefiore. *Feminism and Poetry: Language, Experience, Identity in Women's Writing*, Pandora, London, 1987

Moira Monteith, ed. *Women's Writing: A Challenge to Theory*, Harvester

Press, Brighton, Sussex, 1986

Raoul Mortley. *French Philosophers in Conversation: Derrida, Irigaray, Levinas, Le Doeuff, Schneider, Serres*, Routledge, London, 1991

Laura Mulvey. *Visual and Other Pleasures*, Macmillan, London, 1989

Sally Munt, ed. *New Lesbian Criticism: Literary and Cultural Readings*, Harvester Wheatsheaf, Hemel Hempstead, Herts., 1992

Lynda Nead. *Female Nude: Art, Obscenity and Sexuality*, Routledge, London, 1992

Friedrich Nietzsche. *A Nietzsche Reader*, ed. R.J. Hollingdale, Penguin, London, 1977

Andrea Nye. "Preparing the way for a feminist praxis", *Hypatia*, 1, 1986

D.T. O'Hara, ed. *Why Nietzsche Now?*, Indiana University Press, Bloomington, 1985

Bat-Ami Bar On, ed. *Modern Engendering: Critical Feminist Readings in Modern Western Philosophy*, State University of New York Press, Albany, 1994

Sherry B. Ortner. "Is Female to Male as Nature is to Culture", in M. Evans, ed. *The Woman Question*, Fontana, London, 1982

Carole Pateman & Elizabeth Grosz, eds. *Feminist Challenges*, Allen & Unwin, Sydney, 1986

Michael Payne. *Reading Theory: An Introduction to Lacan, Derrida, and Kristeva*, Blackwell, Oxford, 1993

Mary E. Papke. "The Absent Text: Luce Irigaray's Foray into the Dark Continent of Femininity", *Literature and Psychology*, 32, 1, 1986

Ellen Peel. "The Irony of Women: Reflections of Irigaray", *Cincinnati Romance Review*, 5, 1986

Monique Plaza. ""Phallomorphic power" and the psychology of "woman"", *Ideology and Consciousness*, 4, 1978

E.D. Pribram, ed. *Female Spectators: Looking At Film and TV*, Verso, London, 1988

Leslie Rabine. "Julia Kristeva: Semiotics and Women", *Pacific Coast Philology*, 12, 1977

—. "Écriture Féminine as Metaphor", *Cultural Critique*, 8, Winter, 1987/88

Jean Radford. "Coming to terms: Dorothy Richardson, Modernism and Women", *News From Nowhere*, 7, Winter, 1989

H.L. Radtke & H.J. Stam, eds. *Gender and Power*, Sage, London, 1994

Janice Radway. *Reading the Romance: Feminism and the Representation of Women in Popular Culture*, University of North Carolina Press, Chapel Hill, 1984

J.L. Reich. "Genderfuck: The Law of the Dildo", *Discourse: Journal of Theoretical Studies in Media and Culture*, 15, 1, 1992, 112-127

Philip Rice & Patricia Waugh, eds. *Modern Literary Theory: A Reader*, Arnold, London, 1992

Adrienne Rich. *Of Woman Born: Motherhood as Experience and Institution*, Virago, London, 1977

—. *Blood, Bread and Poetry*, Virago, London, 1980

Michèle Richman. "Sex and Signs: The Language of French Feminist Criticism", *Language and Style*, 13, 4, Autumn, 1980

Jeanne Addison Roberts. *The Shakespearean Wild: Geography, Genus and Gender*, University of Nebraska Press, Lincoln, Nebraska, 1991

Jacqueline Rose. *Sexuality in the Field of Vision*, Verso, London, 1986

Françoise van Rossum-Guyon & Myriam Diaz-Diocaretz, eds. *Hélène Cixous: chemins d'une écriture*, Rodopi, Amsterdam, 1990

Tilde Sankovitch. *French Women Writers and the Book: Myths of Access and Desire*, Syracuse University Press, Syracuse, 1988

Eva Martin Sartori & Dorothy Wynne Zimmerman, eds. *French Women Writers*, University Press, Lincoln, 1994

Janet Sayers. *Biological Politics*, Tavistock, 1982

Naomi Schor. *Breaking the Chain: Women, Theory and French Realist Fiction*, New York, 1985

—. "This essentialism which is not one: coming to grips with Irigaray", *differences*, 1, 2, 1989

—. & Elizabeth Weed, eds. *Differences: More Gender Trouble: Feminism Meets Queer Theory*, 6, 2-3, Indiana University Press, Summer, 1994

Thomas A. Sebeok, ed. *The Tell-Tale Sign: A survey of semiotics*, Peter de Ridder Press, Lisse, Netherlands, 1975

Susan Sellers, ed. *Writing Differences: Readings From the Seminar of Hélène Cixous*, Open University Press, 1988

—. ed. *Delighting the Heart: A Notebook by Women Writers*, Women's Press, London, 1989

—. *Language and Sexual Difference: Feminist Writing in France*, Macmillan, London, 1991

—. ed. *Feminist Criticism: Theory and Practice*, Harvester Wheatsheaf, Hemel Hempstead, Herts., 1991

Morag Shiach. *Hélène Cixous: A Politics of Writing*, Routledge, London, 1991

Elaine Showalter, ed. *The New Feminist Criticism*, Virago, London, 1986

—. ed. *Speaking of Gender*, Routledge, London, 1989

—. *Sexual Anarchy: Gender and Culture at the* Fin de Siècle, Virago, London, 1992

Kaja Silverman. *The Acoustic Mirror: The Female Voice in Psychoanalysis and Cinema*, Indiana University Press, Bloomington, IN, 1988

Dale Spender. *The Writing or the Sex? why you don't have to read women's writing to know it's no good*, Pergamon Press, New York, 1989

Gayatri Chakravorty Spivak: "French feminism in an international frame", *Yale French Studies*, 62, 1981

—. *The Post-Colonial Critic: Interviews, Strategies, Dialogues*, ed. Sarah Harasym, Routledge, London, 1990

George Stambolian & Elaine Marks, eds. *Homosexuality and French Literature: Cultural Contexts/ Critical Texts*, Cornell University Press, Ithaca, 1979

Donna C. Stanton. "Difference on Trial: Critique of the Maternal Metaphor in Cixous, Irigaray, and Kristeva", in N. Miller, 1986

Judith Still & Michael Worton, eds. *Textuality and Sexuality: Reading Theories and Practices*, Manchester University Press, 1993

John Storey, ed. *Cultural Theory and Popular Culture*, Harvester Wheatsheaf, 1994

Susan Rubin Suleiman, ed. *Subversive Intent: Gender, Politics and the Avant-Garde*, Harvard University Press, 1990

—. *Risking Who One Is*, MIT Press, 1995

Chris Weedon. *Feminist Practice and Poststructuralist Theory*, Blackwell, New York, 1987

Helene Wenzel. "The text and body/ politics: an appreciation of Monique Wittig's writings in context", *Feminist Studies*, 7, 1981

Margaret Whitford. "Luce Irigaray and the Female Imaginary: Speaking as a Woman", *Radical Philosophy*, 43, 1986

—. "Luce Irigaray", *Paragraph: The Journal of the Modern Critical Theory Group*, 8, October, 1986

—. "Luce Irigaray's Critique of Rationality", in M. Griffiths, 1988

—. *Luce Irigaray: Philosophy in the Feminine*, Routledge, London, 1991

Helen Wilcox *et al*, eds. *The Body and the Text: Hélène Cixous, Reading and Teaching*, Harvester Wheatsheaf, Hemel Hempstead, Herts., 1990

S. Wilkinson & C. Kitzinger, eds. *Heterosexuality: A Feminism and Psychology Reader*, Sage, London, 1993

Linda Ruth Williams. *Critical Desire: Psychoanalysis and the Literary Subject*, Arnold, London, 1995

—. *Sex in the Head*, Harvester Wheatsheaf, Hemel Hempstead, Herts., 1995

Monique Wittig. *Les Guerillères*, tr. David Le Vay, Viking, New York, 1971

—. "One is Not Born A Woman", *Feminist Issues*, 1, 3, Winter, 1981

—. "Mark of Gender", *Feminist Issues*, 5, 2, 1985

—. *The Lesbian Body*, tr. David Le Vay, Beacon Press, Boston, MA, 1986

—. *The Straight Mind*, Beacon Press, Boston, MA, 1992

Elizabeth Wright, ed. *Feminism and Psychoanalysis: A Critical Dictionary*, Blackwell, Oxford, 1992

Peter Zima, ed. *Semiotics and Dialectics: Ideology and the Text*, Benjamins, Amsterdam, 1981

Jack Zipes. *Don't Bet on the Prince: Contemporary Feminist Fairy Tales in North America and England*, Methuen, New York, 1986

WEBSITES

irigaray.org
kristeva.fr
kristevacircle.org

CRESCENT MOON PUBLISHING

web: www.crmoon.com e-mail: cresmopub@yahoo.co.uk

ARTS, PAINTING, SCULPTURE

The Art of Andy Goldsworthy
Andy Goldsworthy: Touching Nature
Andy Goldsworthy in Close-Up
Andy Goldsworthy: Pocket Guide
Andy Goldsworthy In America
Land Art: A Complete Guide
The Art of Richard Long
Richard Long: Pocket Guide
Land Art In the UK
Land Art in Close-Up
Land Art In the U.S.A.
Land Art: Pocket Guide
Installation Art in Close-Up
Minimal Art and Artists In the 1960s and After
Colourfield Painting
Land Art DVD, TV documentary
Andy Goldsworthy DVD, TV documentary
The Erotic Object: Sexuality in Sculpture From Prehistory to the Present Day
Sex in Art: Pornography and Pleasure in Painting and Sculpture
Postwar Art
Sacred Gardens: The Garden in Myth, Religion and Art
Glorification: Religious Abstraction in Renaissance and 20th Century Art
Early Netherlandish Painting
Leonardo da Vinci
Piero della Francesca
Giovanni Bellini
Fra Angelico: Art and Religion in the Renaissance
Mark Rothko: The Art of Transcendence
Frank Stella: American Abstract Artist
Jasper Johns
Brice Marden
Alison Wilding: The Embrace of Sculpture
Vincent van Gogh: Visionary Landscapes
Eric Gill: Nuptials of God
Constantin Brancusi: Sculpting the Essence of Things
Max Beckmann
Caravaggio
Gustave Moreau
Egon Schiele: Sex and Death In Purple Stockings
Delizioso Fotografico Fervore: Works In Process 1
Sacro Cuore: Works In Process 2
The Light Eternal: J.M.W. Turner
The Madonna Glorified: Karen Arthurs

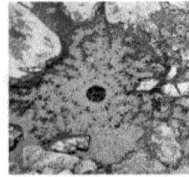

LITERATURE

J.R.R. Tolkien: The Books, The Films, The Whole Cultural Phenomenon
J.R.R. Tolkien: Pocket Guide
Tolkien's Heroic Quest
The *Earthsea* Books of Ursula Le Guin
Beauties, Beasts and Enchantment: Classic French Fairy Tales
German Popular Stories by the Brothers Grimm
Philip Pullman and *His Dark Materials*
Sexing Hardy: Thomas Hardy and Feminism
Thomas Hardy's *Tess of the d'Urbervilles*
Thomas Hardy's *Jude the Obscure*
Thomas Hardy: The Tragic Novels
Love and Tragedy: Thomas Hardy
The Poetry of Landscape in Hardy
Wessex Revisited: Thomas Hardy and John Cowper Powys
Wolfgang Iser: Essays and Interviews
Petrarch, Dante and the Troubadours
Maurice Sendak and the Art of Children's Book Illustration
Andrea Dworkin
Cixous, Irigaray, Kristeva: The *Jouissance* of French Feminism
Julia Kristeva: Art, Love, Melancholy, Philosophy, Semiotics and Psychoanalysis
Hélene Cixous I Love You: The *Jouissance* of Writing
Luce Irigaray: Lips, Kissing, and the Politics of Sexual Difference
Peter Redgrove: Here Comes the Flood
Peter Redgrove: Sex-Magic-Poetry-Cornwall
Lawrence Durrell: Between Love and Death, East and West
Love, Culture & Poetry: Lawrence Durrell
Cavafy: Anatomy of a Soul
German Romantic Poetry: Goethe, Novalis, Heine, Hölderlin
Feminism and Shakespeare
Shakespeare: Love, Poetry & Magic
The Passion of D.H. Lawrence
D.H. Lawrence: Symbolic Landscapes
D.H. Lawrence: Infinite Sensual Violence
Rimbaud: Arthur Rimbaud and the Magic of Poetry
The Ecstasies of John Cowper Powys
Sensualism and Mythology: The Wessex Novels of John Cowper Powys
Amorous Life: John Cowper Powys and the Manifestation of Affectivity (H.W. Fawkner)
Postmodern Powys: New Essays on John Cowper Powys (Joe Boulter)
Rethinking Powys: Critical Essays on John Cowper Powys
Paul Bowles & Bernardo Bertolucci
Rainer Maria Rilke
Joseph Conrad: *Heart of Darkness*
In the Dim Void: Samuel Beckett
Samuel Beckett Goes into the Silence
André Gide: Fiction and Fervour
Jackie Collins and the Blockbuster Novel
Blinded By Her Light: The Love-Poetry of Robert Graves
The Passion of Colours: Travels In Mediterranean Lands
Poetic Forms

POETRY

Ursula Le Guin: Walking In Cornwall
Peter Redgrove: Here Comes The Flood
Peter Redgrove: Sex-Magic-Poetry-Cornwall
Dante: Selections From the Vita Nuova
Petrarch, Dante and the Troubadours
William Shakespeare: Sonnets
William Shakespeare: Complete Poems
Blinded By Her Light: The Love-Poetry of Robert Graves
Emily Dickinson: Selected Poems
Emily Brontë: Poems
Thomas Hardy: Selected Poems
Percy Bysshe Shelley: Poems
John Keats: Selected Poems
Joh n Keats: Poems of 1820
D.H. Lawrence: Selected Poems
Edmund Spenser: Poems
Edmund Spenser: Amoretti
John Donne: Poems
Henry Vaughan: Poems
Sir Thomas Wyatt: Poems
Robert Herrick: Selected Poems
Rilke: Space, Essence and Angels in the Poetry of Rainer Maria Rilke
Rainer Maria Rilke: Selected Poems
Friedrich Hölderlin: Selected Poems
Arseny Tarkovsky: Selected Poems
Arthur Rimbaud: Selected Poems
Arthur Rimbaud: A Season in Hell
Arthur Rimbaud and the Magic of Poetry
Novalis: Hymns To the Night
German Romantic Poetry
Paul Verlaine: Selected Poems
Elizaethan Sonnet Cycles
D.J. Enright: By-Blows
Jeremy Reed: Brigitte's Blue Heart
Jeremy Reed: Claudia Schiffer's Red Shoes
Gorgeous Little Orpheus
Radiance: New Poems
Crescent Moon Book of Nature Poetry
Crescent Moon Book of Love Poetry
Crescent Moon Book of Mystical Poetry
Crescent Moon Book of Elizabethan Love Poetry
Crescent Moon Book of Metaphysical Poetry
Crescent Moon Book of Romantic Poetry
Pagan America: New American Poetry

MEDIA, CINEMA, FEMINISM and CULTURAL STUDIES

J.R.R. Tolkien: The Books, The Films, The Whole Cultural Phenomenon
J.R.R. Tolkien: Pocket Guide
The *Lord of the Rings* Movies: Pocket Guide
The Cinema of Hayao Miyazaki
Hayao Miyazaki: *Princess Mononoke*: Pocket Movie Guide
Hayao Miyazaki: *Spirited Away*: Pocket Movie Guide
Tim Burton : Hallowe'en For Hollywood
Ken Russell
Ken Russell: *Tommy*: Pocket Movie Guide
The Ghost Dance: The Origins of Religion
The Peyote Cult
Cixous, Irigaray, Kristeva: The *Jouissance* of French Feminism
Julia Kristeva: Art, Love, Melancholy, Philosophy, Semiotics and Psychoanalysis
Luce Irigaray: Lips, Kissing, and the Politics of Sexual Difference
Hélene Cixous I Love You: The *Jouissance* of Writing
Andrea Dworkin
'Cosmo Woman': The World of Women's Magazines
Women in Pop Music
HomeGround: The Kate Bush Anthology
Discovering the Goddess (Geoffrey Ashe)
The Poetry of Cinema
The Sacred Cinema of Andrei Tarkovsky
Andrei Tarkovsky: Pocket Guide
Andrei Tarkovsky: *Mirror*: Pocket Movie Guide
Andrei Tarkovsky: *The Sacrifice*: Pocket Movie Guide
Walerian Borowczyk: Cinema of Erotic Dreams
Jean-Luc Godard: The Passion of Cinema
Jean-Luc Godard: *Hail Mary*: Pocket Movie Guide
Jean-Luc Godard: *Contempt*: Pocket Movie Guide
Jean-Luc Godard: *Pierrot le Fou*: Pocket Movie Guide
John Hughes and Eighties Cinema
Ferris Bueller's Day Off: Pocket Movie Guide
Jean-Luc Godard: Pocket Guide
The Cinema of Richard Linklater
Liv Tyler: Star In Ascendance
Blade Runner and the Films of Philip K. Dick
Paul Bowles and Bernardo Bertolucci
Media Hell: Radio, TV and the Press
An Open Letter to the BBC
Detonation Britain: Nuclear War in the UK
Feminism and Shakespeare
Wild Zones: Pornography, Art and Feminism
Sex in Art: Pornography and Pleasure in Painting and Sculpture
Sexing Hardy: Thomas Hardy and Feminism

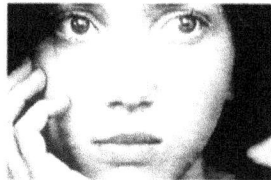

The Light Eternal is a model monograph, an exemplary job. The subject matter of the book is beautifully organised and dead on beam. (Lawrence Durrell)
It is amazing for me to see my work treated with such passion and respect. (Andrea Dworkin)

CRESCENT MOON PUBLISHING
P.O. Box 1312, Maidstone, Kent, ME14 5XU, Great Britain. www.crmoon.com

cresmopub@yahoo.co.uk   www.crescentmoon.org.uk

www.ingramcontent.com/pod-product-compliance
Lightning Source LLC
Chambersburg PA
CBHW062102270326
41931CB00013B/3185